Make Up Your Mind to Be

105 Simple Tips

Josie Varga

A.R.E. Press • Virginia Beach • Virginia

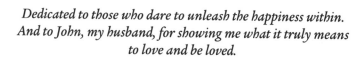

*Dedicated to those who dare to unleash the happiness within.
And to John, my husband, for showing me what it truly means
to love and be loved.*

Contents

Acknowledgments

"Feeling gratitude and not expressing it is like wrapping a present and not giving it."   William Arthur Ward

I AM SO DEEPLY grateful to so many people for had it not been for their positive influence this book would surely have never been born. To start, I would like to thank Dr. Robert Holden for his belief in me. I don't think he realizes how much it has meant to have his support—a man that I deeply admire and respect. Thank you, Robert, for showing me that I can just "Be Happy."

My heartfelt thanks also go out to all the contributors in this book. To His Holiness the Dalai Lama for his kindness and to two members of his office staff, Rinchen Dhondrub and Tenzin Choejor, for allowing me to reprint such a powerful message. Your Holiness the Dalai Lama, your words of wisdom have filled my heart with countless joy.

To the beautiful Debbie Gisonni, you've helped people across the globe live happier and healthier lives. Thank you from the depths of my heart.

To my wonderful friend Geri Jewell, words could never express how happy I am that you came into my life. I am and always will be your biggest fan.

I've known Sue Hershkowitz-Coore for many years now yet she never ceases to amaze me. Sue, you are such a blessing. I don't know what I'd do without you. Your contagious enthusiasm continues to lift my soul.

Marci Shimoff, thank you for teaching me how to be "Happy for No Reason." You are awesome! I am so grateful to you for your support and don't know how I will ever repay you. Also, thank you, Shelly Roby, for staying on top of things. Your help was very much appreciated.

And to the many happiness boosters in my life, my mother and father for giving me the courage to just be me. To my wonderful family and friends, without you, there would be no basis for this book. I love you all.

Erica and Lia, my two beautiful daughters, you are the best gifts life has ever given me. And to John, my wonderful husband, you are my heart and soul.

Lastly, in loving memory of my wonderful godmother Lucy Lobrace. I love you and miss you.

Foreword

HERE'S HOW I FEEL about Josie Varga: I believe Josie is an angel who has taken human form, and a particular one at that, so as to teach us the art of true self-acceptance and happiness.

Josie is an important teacher in my life. Many of her teachings are to be found in the pages of this book, but most of all they are in the example of how she lives. I only have to think of Josie, the challenges she has faced, and the way she lives her days, to receive an instant "spirit boost." Josie helps me to remember the real truth of who I am, what real happiness is, and what is truly important in my life.

Josie Varga's life story will get your attention. On the face of it, Josie has a lot of reasons to be unhappy. Indeed, she has faced a lot of unhappiness in her past. From the moment she was born, Josie has had to face a catalogue of challenges including disability, rejection, discrimination, and abuse. In facing her unhappiness with courage and honesty, Josie has found true happiness.

In Josie's words, "this book is not about teaching you how to be happy. It's about what your soul already knows to be true." Her philosophy of happiness is very similar to what I teach at The Happiness Project, and what I write about in *Happiness NOW* and *Be Happy*.

Like Josie, my experience has taught me that happiness is not an it; happiness is not a thing; happiness is not a destination; happiness is not just a state of mind, and happiness is not just in YOU; happiness is YOU! Happiness is your true nature, and it is what you experience when you allow people like Josie to show you how to listen to your wisdom and follow your joy.

As an added bonus in this book, Josie also introduces you to her friends (who are also angels, like Josie) and to teachers of happiness (like the Dalai Lama and Marci Shimoff). Their insights and tips are a perfect supplement to Josie's teachings. So, I encourage you to get to know Josie, the spirit booster, by turning the pages of this precious book ever so slowly so as to receive the many treasures and blessings therein.

Robert Holden, PhD
London, England
Author, *Be Happy*
www.robertholden.org

Robert Holden and Josie Varga

Introduction

"Most folks are as happy as they make up their minds to be."
Abraham Lincoln

"WE HOLD THESE TRUTHS to be self-evident, that all men are created equal, that they are endowed by their Creator with certain unalienable Rights that among these are Life, Liberty and the pursuit of Happiness." Undoubtedly, this is the most cited line in the Declaration of Independence and one of the best known sentences in American history.

Most of us have grown accustomed to the belief that happiness is something which we need to pursue or strive to obtain. The truth is that the "pursuit of happiness" is quite the paradox. You don't have to go very far to find true happiness as it lies within you. Happiness is your actual state of being, true self, or true nature. Unhappiness, therefore, is ignorance of one's true nature; it is our ego self at work. So, until we realize who we truly are, we will never obtain the happiness that we seek.

Our Founding Fathers knew this. During their era, the word "pursue" meant not to chase after but to practice regularly. Jefferson and the other members of the Continental Congress believed happiness is what God intended for all of us because it is our natural state of being.

Consider what was going on at the time the Declaration of Independence was written: the British were closing in on the American colonies, and we were in the midst of war. Yet, despite everything that was taking place on the outside, happiness was clearly on Jefferson's mind. Happiness is not external but internal. Studies have shown that as Westerners have grown richer over the years, they are no happier. Why?

To answer this question, we need look no further than our children. They live in the moment, never worrying about the things that consume adults. They focus on one thing at a time and do not distress about future events.

Yes, children do get upset, but they don't hang on to that anger or negative emotion. They may be upset about not being able to play with their toys or whatever the case may be, but they are able to let the emotion go as soon as something else grabs their attention. They don't worry about what they are going to do next. The only thing that occupies their minds is being happy in the moment. It is their true nature and it is our true nature.

As we grow older, however, we bury this awareness within because our minds become cluttered with what I like to call "mind chatter." We worry about the bills, the kids, work, etc. The list goes on and on. We are consumed with negative thoughts of fear and desire to the point where we can no longer experience the joy within us. Eventually, these thoughts become our reality.

If we can learn to silence this mind chatter, we can discover happiness once again. Notice here that I didn't say "find happiness." Mystics have long told us that "happiness is inherent in our souls." It is independent of what is going on around us and independent of emotions. This sounds like a contradiction. I mean how can happiness be independent of our emotions? But the truth is when we remove all the negative emotions within, we are left with nothing but happiness. These emotions include: stress, hatred, sadness, depression, envy, jealousy, guilt, doubt, worry, fear, and so many more.

We are not born unhappy; we choose to be unhappy. We are born with an inner peace absent of any negative thoughts. We knew only compassion, joy, and love. There was no judgment, only acceptance. And this acceptance is what allowed that inner peace to grow. As Gandhi once said, "Be the peace you wish to see in the world."

True happiness is possible at all times, no matter what the circumstances in your life. It doesn't matter how much money you have or how many material things you own. The fact is research has shown that the wealthy are not necessarily happier than the poor. On the contrary, many people have become unhappy once they struck it rich. If you look for happiness, you will never be happy. Ironically, the more you chase after it, the further you are from it.

Material things don't make us happy. They bring us only pleasure. There is a difference. Pleasure is an enjoyment brought on by outside incentives. There are many things that can bring us pleasure like buying a new house, getting a college degree, meeting with friends, making love, etc. Pleasure requires something to happen in order for you to experience it. This is not the case with happiness. While pleasure is external, happiness is internal. Something that brings us pleasure will not necessarily make us happy.

You might be saying, "Well, that is easy for you to say; you've probably lived a trouble-free and comfortable life." Nothing could be further from the truth. Allow me to tell you a little about myself.

My father and his four siblings grew up poor on a farm in Italy, escaping to the United States in search of the American Dream. Although my mother, who was born in Partinico, Sicily, did not grow up on a farm, bread and meat were a special treat in her house as they were provided only on special occasions. My parents married and had three children of which I was the youngest and was named after my maternal grandmother Josephine Oliveri.

My family was surprised by my premature arrival at 7½ months with reddish hair and big blue eyes, looking nothing like my dark-haired, brown-eyed brother and sister. But even more surprising was the realization that their little girl had a disability. I was born with cerebral palsy (CP), which is a non-progressive condition caused by brain damage characterized by muscular or motor impairment. CP is often accompanied by problems with sensation, perception, and speech.

No two cases of CP are exactly alike, and cases range from extremely severe to relatively mild. I am very fortunate as my case is very mild. However, I still spent time in a wheelchair, grew up wearing leg braces, and still suffer from a speech impediment as well as severe bilateral hearing loss.

As a little girl, I can remember watching the neighborhood kids playing in the street and wondering if I were ever going to be one of them. Would they ever accept me or would they continue to poke fun at me and the way I walked? Something told me that I was going to be subjected to their mockery for a long time, and I was. Through it all, the one thing that I craved more than anything else in the world was happiness. I craved it with a passion. But how could I be happy when I was not accepted by the outside world? How could I be happy when I struggled to get by with my level of hearing and fell down almost daily from the lack of balance in my legs?

My teenage years were especially difficult as kids continued to make fun of me and even physically abused me. Again, I was absolutely miserable. If it weren't for the support of my family and friends, I don't know what I would have done. But if you were to ask my parents how I was as a baby, they would tell you that I was the happiest thing on the face of this earth, always smiling, always content and happy. So what happened?

Somewhere along the line, I let people dictate my feelings. I believed, like many others, that people determine our happiness. We can all attest to this when we make comments like "he makes me so happy." The fact is you make yourself happy. No one else can do that for you. Yet many of us have been unhappy for so long that we have no clue how to get back to our original state of happiness—our true self. We get so caught up in everything that is going on around us that we develop a form of amnesia and have no idea who or what we are anymore. The good news is your true inherent state is still there and will always be there. It's who you are. You need only to take the time to uncover it once again.

It is finding this inner peace that supersedes anything physical on this earth and brings all of us to a state of joy and contentment where we can once again meet with true understanding. This is a gradual process that takes time and cannot happen overnight. I didn't wake up one morning and suddenly decide to be happy. I came to many realizations in life which eventually changed my view of this precious world and the people around me. For one thing, I realized just how rich I am. There's a Buddhist proverb that states, "He who is satisfied with what he has is rich." I couldn't agree more.

I changed my thoughts and hence, my life. As I said before, our thoughts create our reality. Think of it this way: everything that you do, you've thought of first. Well, then, what exactly is reality? Do you believe that everything you see is real? If it's real, it's only because you've made it real. Everything that we see is a manifestation of the way we think. 50 percent of our attitudes and beliefs are said to be learned by the time we are four-years-old. Over the next ten years by the age of fourteen, psychologists believe we learn another 40 percent of our beliefs.

This explains why we forget our inherent true nature and thus lose touch with our state of happiness within. Consider the fact that the human brain is estimated to be capable of processing one hundred trillion instructions per second. The fastest super computer in the world, known as the Roadrunner, is only about ten times faster than the human brain. But the actual computational power of the human brain is hard to pinpoint because it is also controlling the sensory, aural, and visual input of millions of nerve cells throughout the body. Let's not forget, too, that the brain is also monitoring oxygen, the heart, breathing, etc.

Nerve cells constantly send messages to your brain telling you, for instance, whether your coffee is hot or cold or whether you feel happy or sad. The good news is we choose which of these messages we want to focus on at any given time.

So, then, can we change our reality? Absolutely, we can by simply changing the way we think and what we choose to focus on. These choices then precede action and reaction. For example, say I choose to focus on the fact that one of my friends lied to me in the past, I may then become upset and opt not to speak to this person again. Let's try this from another angle.

Now, say this same friend lied to me, but I choose to instead focus on his good traits. I may then laugh his action off and continue on with the friendship for many years to come. How we respond to the past will continue to control what happens in the future unless we learn to take control of the present by changing the way we think.

This book was born not out of my desire to be happy but out of the realization that I am already and will always be. Please don't misunderstand me here. I am not saying that I don't experience times of unhappiness and distress. Being happy does not mean you are never unhappy. I have been there many times and will be there time and time again. After the birth of my daughter Erica, I was diagnosed with melanoma, the worst form of skin cancer. Since then, I've had so many moles surgically removed from my body that I've often felt like a piece of Swiss cheese. I've also feared that I would not be around to see my children grow up.

So again, I am by no means saying that I don't experience negative emotions such as anger, doubt, or unhappiness. My ego self still often comes to the surface. What I am saying is that I have totally accepted myself and who I am.

This is the most crucial step on the road to happiness. Without total acceptance, there can be no happiness. In my case, it took me a long time to accept myself with all my so-called "imperfections." Growing up with a disability was not easy and continues to be difficult today. But I would never change anything about my life. I accept myself and love myself as I am.

It is difficult for many people to love themselves. It seems almost egotistical or conceited. Yet, you will never know your true nature unless you know love. You will never know love unless you give love. It goes full circle because, once again, love and happiness are our true nature.

Total acceptance is so important that I'd like you to try an exercise before we get further into this book. Put this book down and go look yourself in the mirror. I mean really, truly look in the mirror and please be honest with yourself.

The following are the 10 W's of happiness. Please answer the following:
1. Who am I?
2. What do I need?
3. What are my desires?
4. What and who makes me happy?
5. What makes me unhappy?
6. What do I have?
7. What do I want?
8. What am I grateful for?

9. What could I do to be happy right now?
10. What does happiness mean to me?

Your answers to these questions will dictate what you get out of this book. So, again, please take the time to reflect on your answers. If you were to ask me who am I, I would tell you first and foremost that I am the mother of two beautiful girls. This is what is most important to me in my life.

Question four is another significant one. What and who makes me happy? If your grandchildren make you happy, then spend more time with them even if it means getting on a plane and flying across the country. If dancing brings out the happiness within, then don't walk, dance. Do more of whatever makes you happy NOW!

How about what do I need? Well, I used to think that I needed a bigger house. Truthfully, my family and I are pretty cramped in our home. But the fact is I don't need a bigger house, I want a bigger house. There is a big difference between our wants and needs. Too often people don't understand the difference because they are too busy concentrating on what they don't have rather than what they do have. You get the picture. It really helps to put things into perspective.

Look at it this way, going back to the need for a bigger house above, what happens when you get the bigger house? People are constantly falling into the "I'll be happy when" scenario only to realize that they are no happier when they reach their goal. Until you realize that happiness is your true self, you will forever be searching for more. And I guarantee you that you will always come up short.

Once you can appreciate what you already have in your life, you will attract more of it into your life. As Marci Shimoff, best-selling author and featured teacher in *The Secret*, explains later in this book, "Like attracts like. What you appreciate, appreciates. Whenever you appreciate the happiness that already exists in your life, you attract more of it into your life."

If your appreciation expands, you will continue to bring happiness to others and hence bring it back to yourself. As the great American psychic Edgar Cayce noted, "Happiness is a state of mind by giving to others."

This book is not about teaching you how to be happy. It's about what your soul already knows to be true. The following Spirit Boosters are simple tips that can help you choose happiness by changing your thoughts and helping you to focus on the positive. Studies have shown that doing so actually changes the chemistry of your brain. In one such experiment, patients suffering from depression either were treated with drugs or cognitive-behavior therapy. The results revealed that each set of patients experienced completely different changes in the same area of the brain. In other words, positive thinking will actually bring about changes to the makeup of your brain the same way medication can.

I encourage you to use the PT (positive thoughts) Journal in the back of this book. Keeping such a journal will help you develop an attitude about gratitude. How you feel about happiness affects everything else in your life (all of your relationships, decisions, goals, desires . . . everything!).

Continually emphasizing the things you are grateful for trains your brain to concentrate on the positives in your life rather than the negative. So, while individually some of the Spirit Boosters in this book may seem almost trivial, together and over time these steps are transformative as they can work to bring our true nature to the surface once again.

The Happiness PPF Pre-Test

Happiness means different things to different people, but overall how we think about ourselves, our place in this world and how we act is what differentiates happy people from the less happy people.

Below is what I call the PPF Test. There is, of course, no right or wrong answer. This questionnaire is meant to help you gauge your happiness level by testing your PPF which refers to being:

- Accepting of the **P**AST
- Actively Happy in the **P**RESENT and
- Optimistic about the **F**UTURE

Think each question through and be honest. You will have the opportunity to take this again later to determine whether or not your attitude has changed.

TEST YOUR HAPPINESS *PPF LEVEL

I am happy.
Less True ☺ ☺ ☺ ☺ ☺ More True

I focus on the positive in any situation.
Less True ☺ ☺ ☺ ☺ ☺ More True

I say I love you at least once a day.
Less True ☺ ☺ ☺ ☺ ☺ More True

I make time for friends and family.
Less True ☺ ☺ ☺ ☺ ☺ More True

My life is purposeful.
Less True ☺ ☺ ☺ ☺ ☺ More True

I accept the past.
Less True ☺ ☺ ☺ ☺ ☺ More True

I am optimistic about the future.
Less True ☺ ☺ ☺ ☺ ☺ More True

I can do anything I put my mind to.
Less True ☺ ☺ ☺ ☺ ☺ More True

I give hugs as often as I can.
Less True ☺ ☺ ☺ ☺ ☺ More True

I am honest with myself and the way I feel.
Less True ☺ ☺ ☺ ☺ ☺ More True

I seek out positive people.
Less True ☺ ☺ ☺ ☺ ☺ More True

I weed out the people who drag me down.

Less True ☺ ☺ ☺ ☺ ☺ More True

I wake up with a positive thought every morning.

Less True ☺ ☺ ☺ ☺ ☺ More True

I believe everything happens for a reason.

Less True ☺ ☺ ☺ ☺ ☺ More True

I have fun often enough.

Less True ☺ ☺ ☺ ☺ ☺ More True

I deserve to be happy.

Less True ☺ ☺ ☺ ☺ ☺ More True

I accept myself for who I am.

Less True ☺ ☺ ☺ ☺ ☺ More True

It doesn't matter what others think of me.

Less True ☺ ☺ ☺ ☺ ☺ More True

This world is a beautiful place.

Less True ☺ ☺ ☺ ☺ ☺ More True

I smile often.

Less True ☺ ☺ ☺ ☺ ☺ More True

I surprise my friends for no reason.

Less True ☺ ☺ ☺ ☺ ☺ More True

I am fun to be around.

Less True ☺ ☺ ☺ ☺ ☺ More True

I don't worry about things I have no control over.

Less True   ☺   ☺   ☺   ☺   ☺   More True

I am exactly where I should be in life.

Less True   ☺   ☺   ☺   ☺   ☺   More True

I laugh just because it makes me feel good.

Less True   ☺   ☺   ☺   ☺   ☺   More True

I appreciate my old friends and am always open to making new ones.

Less True   ☺   ☺   ☺   ☺   ☺   More True

I can easily forgive others.

Less True   ☺   ☺   ☺   ☺   ☺   More True

I am a good person and always try to help others.

Less True   ☺   ☺   ☺   ☺   ☺   More True

*PPF refers to being accepting of the PAST, actively happy in the PRESENT, and optimistic about the FUTURE.

Tips 1 to 20

☀ 1 Recognize Life as a Gift

If you really want to lift your spirit, you must realize first and foremost that life is a gift. It is not something to be taken for granted. I know because I am very guilty of doing just that. We all do. We get so caught up in our day-to-day routines that we don't stop to realize how lucky we truly are.

For me, it took the idea of death to awaken my very spirit and make me realize how precious life really is. I was diagnosed with melanoma, the worst form of skin cancer, at the age of thirty-five. Up until then, I never took my time too seriously. Nowadays, I appreciate everything about my life: my family, my friends, my ability to write, the beautiful evergreens in my backyard, etc. Ironically, being diagnosed with a potentially fatal cancer taught me about the value of life.

☀ 2 Slow Down

There's a Taoist saying which states that the emptiness inside of a jug is what makes it useful. At first, I didn't understand what this meant. But then I equated the saying to the significance of making time for the important things in life.

If a jug is full, we can't put anything else in it. Likewise, if we speed through life going from one routine to the next, we won't have the time to realize what's in front of us; we can't just be content and enjoy life because we are constantly struggling to maintain it.

Have you ever noticed that when you are on vacation, time seems to slow down? The days seem a little longer. The reason for this is simple: when we slow down, our lives slow down too, and we have more time to appreciate life and just be happy.

☀ 3 Open Yourself to Intimacy

Most people think of sexual relations when they hear the word intimacy. And, in fact, being intimate with another individual can mean that you are sexually active with that person. However, it can also mean the closeness you feel to a friend.

Most people are afraid to seek intimacy because they are afraid of getting hurt. But the joy that you stand to gain from opening up to another person; the warmth that you will feel from that mutual bond is well worth the risk. After all, as Alfred Lord Tennyson said, " 'Tis better to have loved and lost than never to have loved at all."

☀ 4 Stop Believing Money Will Buy You Happiness

Richard Friedman once said, "Money will buy you a fine dog, but it will not make it wag its tail." Although many are quick to assume that having more money will make them feel happy, research has shown time and time again that the relationship between happiness and money is, in fact, very slim.

Sure, you may experience a feeling of joy after finding out you've won the lottery, for example, but this moment of bliss is not long–term and does not contribute to your overall level of happiness. In fact, excessive wealth can cause depression for those who are not accustomed to it.

I'm not saying that I wouldn't mind a little extra cash. God knows I could use it! But let's say I had three million dollars and I didn't have my husband or my children to love me, the money might make my life easier, but it certainly would not make me happier.

☀ **5** Exercise Your Mood

Everyone knows that participating in some form of physical exercise is important for our physical well-being. Exercise has long been known to reduce the risk of heart disease, high blood pressure, and high cholesterol. It has even been noted to reduce the risk of certain forms of cancer.

But what many people don't realize, however, is that exercise is important to our psychological well-being as well. It helps to reduce anxiety, stress, and depression. So make the time to exercise. You can benefit substantially by exercising thirty to sixty minutes, three to five times a week. For those of you, who are thinking that you just don't have the time, try taking the stairs at work instead of the elevator; walk as much as you can; do yard work at home, etc. As they say, "Anything is better than nothing."

☀ **6** Laugh Out Loud

"Humor might not have saved my life, but it definitely made my life," says Michael Aronin. "At various turns, it has made my life bearable; at others, remarkable; at still others, joyful, committed, and amazing." Michael, a comedian and motivational speaker with cerebral palsy, definitely knows the benefits of laughter.

Not only does laughter make you feel good, but it also reduces stress, lowers blood pressure, and boosts our immune system by raising levels of infection-fighting cells in our body. Studies have shown that laughter releases endorphins which are the body's natural painkillers. So laugh as much as you can. Laughter is contagious; you'll make other feel good too!

☀ 7 Organize Your House

You have a "junk" drawer in the kitchen that you've been meaning to clean and a closet jam-packed with clothes that you've wanted to organize for months. Your basement is cluttered with boxes filled with things you no longer need or want. Well, now's the time to finally take a moment to bring a little order to your life. You'll be surprised how good you feel.

I share my desk with my husband and two young daughters. It is absolutely impossible for my desk not to become piled high with everything from coloring books and bills to my work. Needless to say, I am constantly cleaning my desk because I find it impossible to concentrate with clutter all around me. It drives me absolutely crazy.

Someday I would love to hire a *feng shui* expert to help me organize my home. *Feng shui* is an ancient Chinese practice of arranging space and placing furniture to be in harmony with the environment. Some believe that this practice has an effect on everything from physical and mental health to wealth and material gain.

Figure out what has been bothering you and work on organizing it. I promise to do the same.

☀ 8 Don't be Afraid to Say "I Love You"

I've never been one to hold my feelings inside. After only three weeks of dating my husband, I blurted out, "John, I love you," as tears streamed down my face. He looked at me overjoyed to hear those words yet disappointed that he wasn't the one to say them first. For months afterward, every time he told me that he loved me, I would reply, "Yes, but I said it first." It would always make us laugh.

Like John, many people are afraid to say "I love you." They are either afraid that it's either too soon to express this sentiment or perhaps that the other person will not say it back. Well, I can understand these fears, but I am going to argue that it is well worth the risk of getting hurt. However, I don't believe it is ever too soon to say "I love you." If it were too soon, then you wouldn't be feeling these emotions in the first place.

Let that special someone in your life know exactly how you feel. Pay close attention to your heart. Not only is it therapeutic, but it will also let you know exactly where you stand in the relationship.

☼ 9 Show How You Feel

As the old adage goes, "Actions speak louder than words." I must say that I couldn't agree more. What good is telling someone that you care if you don't act like you do? It doesn't matter how long you've known someone, we all need reassurance from time to time. Reassurances can be as simple as sending a card or setting aside time to take your friend out to dinner.

One of my closest friends once blurted out, "You don't care." Her words shocked me. After many years of friendship, I couldn't understand why and how she could possibly think that I didn't care about her. But then I realized that I had been so caught up in my work and spending time with my new friends in my hometown that I had neglected our friendship.

☼ 10 Light Some Candles

Did you know that smell is the most heightened of all our senses? Research has shown that what we smell has a tremendous impact on how we feel, both mentally and physically. Perhaps the smell of freshly baked chocolate chip cookies reminds you of your childhood. Or maybe the smell of the brisk ocean breeze helps you to relax as you take a stroll on the beach.

The scents from essential oils are believed to help relieve many stress-related ailments as well as promote recovery of others including colds, insomnia, migraines, and muscle pains. For example, lavender oil is said to help you sleep while rosemary is noted to promote muscle relaxation. There are several varieties of scented candles and oils on the market. So have fun finding the scents that work best for you!

☀ 11 Quiet Your Mind

The act of meditation comes with many benefits including stress and anxiety reduction. Relaxing and quieting the mind can even reduce the risk of heart disease and other illnesses. There are various ways to meditate, but I'd like to share a simple one with only three steps.

1. Find a relaxed and peaceful location. While some prefer absolute silence, others prefer soft background music. Whatever works for you is fine.
2. Next find a comfortable position that you will be able to sit in for an extended period of time without tiring. This could be on the floor or on the sofa.
3. Now, once you're comfortable, close your eyes and focus on something. Perhaps, you might focus on a memory shared with a loved one. Or you can repeat a positive phrase over and over in your mind such as, "I am loved." Relax and take a deep breath each time you say it. Release negative energy (fear, worry, anger, sadness) with each exhalation and take in positive energy (joy, happiness, contentment) with each inhalation.

Try not to get discouraged if you don't feel the benefits immediately. It may take some time and trial-and-error to find the meditation technique that's right for you.

☀ 12 Ask Yourself Some Tough Questions

Sometimes in life, you not only have to ask yourself some tough questions but you also have to answer them honestly. Questions like: What do I really want out of life? What bothers me the most? What do I wish I could change? Am I truly happy with my marriage/relationship? What do I need to make my life happier?

The key here is to be totally honest with yourself. Your answers will help you better understand who you truly are. Hence, you will be able to make better choices that create happiness and contentment for you.

☼ 13 Draw on Your Strengths; Acknowledge Your Weaknesses

We all know what our strengths and weaknesses are. But far too often, instead of drawing on our strengths, we tend to concentrate on the things we cannot do. I grew up with cerebral palsy. As a result of my disability, I have many weaknesses. As a little girl, it bothered me to no end that I could never go ice skating with my friends. I tried several times, but I just could not maintain my balance on skates.

Then one day I said to myself, "You may not be able to do a lot of things, but you can also do a lot more than some people." After all, I had a disability. Yet I could walk and even run on my own. I could ride my bike. And I was a good writer. Through my writing and my imagination, in fact, I was able to do anything that I wanted to do. Whenever you find yourself confronting one of your weaknesses, look beyond it and find happiness in your strengths.

Think of the things you can do and not the things you can't do. Similarly, look at the things you have done in your life and not the things you have yet to do. Remember, your attitude is what makes all the difference.

☼ 14 Temper Your Expectations of Others

I must admit that this concept has been extremely difficult for me. We all expect certain things from our family and friends. But what I've found over the years is the more I expect from others, the more I'm apt to be disappointed.

In 2000, when I was diagnosed with skin cancer, I felt like I had the weight of the Empire State Building on my shoulders. I was miserably depressed. When I got the news, I expected certain things from my friends. I wanted everyone to stop what they were doing and run over to lend me a shoulder to cry on.

Very few did what I expected. So I found myself mad and resentful of all my other friends. As time went on, however, I realized that just because my other friends did not respond the way I had expected them to didn't mean that they didn't care. Everyone has his own way of dealing with things.

I came to realize that it's not fair to expect my friends or family to drop everything they were doing and run to me. I learned not to expect too much. This way I can continue to appreciate them regardless of whatever happens in my life.

☼ 15 Believe in Yourself

Sometimes you believe in everything and everybody except the person who is the most important: you!

No one will believe in you if **you** don't believe in you. It has to start with you. Get reacquainted with yourself. Know who you are and why you are that way. Tell yourself that you can accomplish anything. Reflect on how far you've come in life and think about where you want to go from here. Know what you want and make a feasible plan to make it happen.

If you believe in yourself, life becomes so much easier because you will fear less and achieve more. You will be more open to see and to take advantage of opportunities when they come up.

☼ 16 Tune into Nature

Millions of years ago, *Homo sapiens* first walked about the earth's natural terrain barefoot. Their bodies were so in tune with nature that they could easily walk over stones and tree branches. Doing so not only helped them survive during those primitive times, but it helped them develop a deep connection to the earth and fostered spiritual well-being.

I love the feeling of calmness that I experience when I walk on the beach barefoot. The sand and pebbles caressing my toes, heighten my sense of awareness, and make me feel like I'm one with the earth. Try it. Of course, you don't have to walk on the beach. If you prefer, it can be the grass in your backyard or even the rocks and dirt at the local park.

☼ 17 Embrace Change

As they say, there are two things that are certain in life: death and taxes. Well, I think one more thing should be added to the equation and that is change. It is not only everywhere, it is inevitable. There's not a thing we can do about it.

For example, we are all growing older every day. Again, there's not a thing we can do about how many years we have on this earth. Yet, people spend billions of dollars on cosmetics and plastic surgery in a desperate attempt to turn back the clock. Ironically, the stress that this sometimes causes can actually have the opposite effect. So why waste your much-needed energy trying to resist change? Instead, embrace and accept it.

☼ 18 Know that Things Are Not Always What They Seem

Things are not always what they seem. It sounds pretty logical and easy to accept, right? Well, no, not exactly. Realizing and accepting the fact that things aren't always how we perceive them is a very difficult milestone to pass. Let me give you an example.

I was born with severe bilateral hearing loss. When my husband and I first moved into our current house, we were amazed at how wonderful our neighbors were. Everyone was very friendly and would frequently yell out greetings from their front lawns. The only problem was that I frequently had no idea they were speaking to me. I was perceived as snobbish because I seemed not to want to engage in conversation. But the truth was I was very anxious to get to know my new neighbors, I just couldn't always hear them.

When I finally got around to telling my neighbors that I was hearing impaired, they all gave me this look like "Oh, so that's why you ignored me the other day." The lesson here is to always give people second chances. If a friend was rude to you the other day, maybe it had nothing at all to do with you. Maybe she was going through some tough times. Ask for an explanation. Don't just assume things are one way or the other.

☀ 19 Have a PMA— Positive Mental Attitude

As I was growing up, my big brother Michael would often tell me whenever I was down or upset about something, "Remember, Josie you have to have a PMA." When I was a kid, I used to stare back at him like I thought he was crazy. Today as an adult, however, I realize how wise my brother's words were.

The fact of the matter is we can't control everything that happens in this life; however, we can control how we respond to what happens. We can choose to focus on the positive.

When we do so, we give our spirit a boost. And when our spirits are high, we are better able to deal with whatever adversities may come our way.

Studies have shown that those who are positive tend to live longer and better lives. So, as my brother always used to say, remember to have a PMA.

☀ 20 Be Spontaneous; Have Fun

As I write this, I am nine months shy of my forty-third birthday. The truth is, however, mentally I don't feel any different than I did when I was twenty-five. The difference is now I am a mother and have a lot more responsibility than I did in my younger days. I am definitely not as carefree as I once was. But there are times when I long for my carefree days. I just want to be a kid again.

On those days, I may call a few of my friends and arrange a girls' night out or do something fun and spontaneous with my husband. Or maybe I'll call Lisa or Adriana, two of my oldest childhood friends, and talk about the old times. The years never truly pass between old friends; they only sweeten and become more memorable.

His Holiness the Dalai Lama

The following was reprinted with permission from the office of His Holiness the Dalai Lama at www.dalailama.com

One Great Question

ONE GREAT QUESTION UNDERLIES our experience, whether we think about it consciously or not: What is the purpose of life? I have considered this question and would like to share my thoughts in the hope that they may be of direct, practical benefit to those who read them.

I believe that the purpose of life is to be happy. From the moment of birth, every human being wants happiness and does not want suffering. Neither social conditioning nor education nor ideology affects this. From the very core of our being, we simply desire contentment. I don't know whether the universe, with its countless galaxies, stars and planets, has a deeper meaning or not, but at the very least, it is clear that we humans who live on this earth face the task of making a happy life for ourselves. Therefore, it is important to discover what will bring about the greatest degree of happiness.

How to Achieve Happiness

For a start, it is possible to divide every kind of happiness and suffering into two main categories: mental and physical. Of the two, it is the mind that exerts the greatest influence on most of us. Unless we are either gravely ill or deprived of basic necessities, our physical condition plays a secondary role in life. If the body is content, we virtually ignore it. The mind, however, registers every event, no matter how small. Hence we should devote our most serious efforts to bringing about mental peace. From my own limited experience I have found that the greatest degree of inner tranquility comes from the development of love and compassion. The more we care for the happiness of others, the greater our own sense of well-being becomes. Cultivating a close, warm-hearted feeling for others automatically puts the mind at ease. This helps remove whatever fears or insecurities we may have and gives us the strength to cope with any obstacles we encounter. It is the ultimate source of success in life. As long as we live in this world we are bound to encounter problems. If, at such times, we lose hope and become discouraged, we diminish our ability to face difficulties. If, on the other hand, we remember that it is not just ourselves but everyone who has to undergo suffering, this more realistic perspective will increase our determination and capacity to overcome troubles. Indeed, with this attitude, each new obstacle can be seen as yet another valuable opportunity to improve our mind! Thus we can strive gradually to become more compassionate, that is we can develop both genuine sympathy for others' suffering and the will to help remove their pain. As a result, our own serenity and inner strength will increase.

Our Need for Love

Ultimately, the reason why love and compassion bring the greatest happiness is simply that our nature cherishes them above all else. The need for love lies at the very foundation of human existence. It results from the profound interdependence we all share with one another.

However capable and skillful an individual may be, left alone, he or she will not survive. However vigorous and independent one may feel during the most prosperous periods of life, when one is sick or very young or very old, one must depend on the support of others.

Independence, of course, is a fundamental law of nature. Not only higher forms of life but also many of the smallest insects are social beings who, without any religion, law or education, survive by mutual cooperation based on an innate recognition of their interconnectedness. The most subtle level of material phenomena is also governed by interdependence. All phenomena from the planet we inhabit to the oceans, clouds, forests and flowers that surround us, arise in independence upon subtle patterns of energy. Without their proper interaction, they dissolve and decay.

It is because our own human existence is so dependent on the help of others that our need for love lies at the very foundation of our existence. Therefore we need a genuine sense of responsibility and a sincere concern for the welfare of others.

We have to consider what we human beings really are. We are not like machine-made objects. If we are merely mechanical entities, then machines themselves could alleviate all of our sufferings and fulfill our needs. However, since we are not solely material creatures, it is a mistake to place all our hopes for happiness on external development alone. Instead, we should consider our origins and nature to discover what we require.

Leaving aside the complex question of the creation and evolution of our universe, we can at least agree that each of us is the product of our own parents. In general, our conception took place not just in the context of sexual desire but from our parents' decision to have a child. Such decisions are founded on responsibility and altruism—the parents' compassionate commitment to care of their child until it is able to take care of itself. Thus, from the very moment of our conception, our parents' love is directly in our creation.

Moreover, we are completely dependent upon our mothers' care from the earliest stages of our growth. According to some scientists, a pregnant woman's mental state, be it calm or agitated has a direct physical effect on her unborn child.

The expression of love is also very important at the time of birth. Since the very first thing we do is suck milk from our mothers' breast, we naturally feel close to her, and she must feel love for us in order to feed us properly; if she feels anger or resentment her milk may not flow freely. Then there is the critical period of brain development from the time of birth up to at least the age of three or four, during which time loving physical contact is the single most important factor for the normal growth of the child. If the child is not held, hugged, cuddled, or loved, its development will be impaired and its brain will not mature properly.

Since a child cannot survive without the care of others, love is its most important nourishment. The happiness of childhood, the allaying of the child's many fears and the healthy development of its self–confidence all depend directly upon love.

Nowadays, many children grow up in unhappy homes. If they do not receive proper affection, in later life they will rarely love their parents and, not infrequently, will find it hard to love others. This is very sad.

As children grow older and enter school, their need for support must be met by their teachers. If a teacher not only imparts academic education but also assumes responsibility for preparing students for life, his or her pupils will feel trust and respect and what has been taught will leave an indelible impression on their minds. On the other hand, subjects taught by a teacher who does not show true concern for his or her students' overall well–being will be regarded as temporary and not retained for long.

Similarly, if one is sick and being treated in hospital by a doctor who evinces a warm human feeling, one feels at ease and the doctors' desire to give the best possible care is itself curative, irrespective of the degree of his or her technical skill. On the other hand, if one's doctor lacks human feeling and displays an unfriendly expression, impatience or casual disregard, one will feel anxious, even if he or she is the most highly qualified doctor and the disease has been correctly diagnosed and the right medication prescribed. Inevitably, patients' feelings make a difference to the quality and completeness of their recovery.

Even when we engage in ordinary conversation in everyday life, if someone speaks with human feeling we enjoy listening, and respond accordingly; the whole conversation becomes interesting, however unimportant the topic may be. On the other hand, if a person speaks coldly or harshly, we feel uneasy and wish for a quick end to the interaction. From the least to the most important event, the affection and respect of others are vital for our happiness.

Recently I met a group of scientists in America who said that the rate of mental illness in their country was quite high—around 12 percent of the population. It became clear during our discussion that the main cause of depression was not a lack of material necessities but a deprivation of the affection of the others. So, as you can see from everything I have written so far, one thing seems clear to me: whether or not we are consciously aware of it, from the day we are born, the need for human affection is in our very blood. Even if the affection comes from an animal or someone we would normally consider an enemy, both children and adults will naturally gravitate towards it.

I believe that no one is born free from the need for love. And this demonstrates that, although some modern schools of thought seek to do so, human beings cannot be defined as solely physical. No material object, however beautiful or valuable, can make us feel loved, because our deeper identity and true character lie in the subjective nature of the mind.

Developing Compassion

Some of my friends have told me that, while love and compassion are marvelous and good, they are not really very relevant. Our world, they say, is not a place where such beliefs have much influence or power. They claim that anger and hatred are so much a part of human nature that humanity will always be dominated by them. I do not agree.

We humans have existed in our present form for about a hundred-thousand years. I believe that if during this time the human mind had been primarily controlled by anger and hatred, our overall population would have decreased. But today, despite all our wars, we find that the human population is greater than ever. This clearly indicates to me that love and compassion predominate in the world.

And this is why unpleasant events are "news"; compassionate activities are so much part of daily life that they are taken for granted and, therefore, largely ignored.

So far I have been discussing mainly the mental benefits of compassion, but it contributes to good physical health as well. According to my personal experience, mental stability and physical well-being are directly related. Without question, anger and agitation make us more susceptible to illness. On the other hand, if the mind is tranquil and occupied with positive thoughts, the body will not easily fall prey to disease.

But of course it is also true that we all have an innate self-centeredness that inhibits our love for others. So, since we desire the true happiness that is brought about by only a calm mind, and since such peace of mind is brought about by only a compassionate attitude, how can we develop this? Obviously, it is not enough for us simply to think about how nice compassion is! We need to make a concerted effort to develop it; we must use all the events of our daily life to transform our thoughts and behavior.

First of all, we must be clear about what we mean by compassion. Many forms of compassionate feeling are mixed with desire and attachment. For instance, the love parents feel for their child is often strongly associated with their own emotional needs, so it is not fully compassionate. Again, in marriage, the love between husband and wife—particularly at the beginning, when each partner still may not know the other's deeper character very well depends more on attachment than genuine love. Our desire can be so strong that the person to whom we are attached appears to be good, when in fact he or she is very negative. In addition, we have a tendency to exaggerate small positive qualities. Thus when one partner's attitude changes, the other partner is often disappointed and his or her attitude changes too. This is an indication that love has been motivated more by personal need than by genuine care for the other individual.

True compassion is not just an emotional response but a firm commitment founded on reason. Therefore, a truly compassionate attitude towards others does not change even if they behave negatively.

Of course, developing this kind of compassion is not at all easy! As a start, let us consider the following facts:

Whether people are beautiful and friendly or unattractive and disruptive, ultimately they are human beings, just like oneself. Like oneself, they want happiness and do not want suffering. Furthermore, their right to overcome suffering and be happy is equal to one's own. Now, when you recognize that all beings are equal in both their desire for happiness and their right to obtain it, you automatically feel empathy and closeness for them. Through accustoming your mind to this sense of universal altruism, you develop a feeling of responsibility for others: the wish to help them actively overcome their problems. Nor is this wish selective; it applies equally to all. As long as they are human beings experiencing pleasure and pain just as you do, there is no logical basis to discriminate between them or to alter your concern for them if they behave negatively.

Let me emphasize that it is within your power, given patience and time, to develop this kind of compassion. Of course, our self-centeredness, our distinctive attachment to the feeling of an independent, self existent "I", works fundamentally to inhibit our compassion. Indeed, true compassion can be experienced only when this type of self-grasping is eliminated. But this does not mean that we cannot start and make progress now.

How Can We Start?

We should begin by removing the greatest hindrances to compassion: anger and hatred. As we all know, these are extremely powerful emotions and they can overwhelm our entire mind. Nevertheless, they can be controlled. If, however, they are not, these negative emotions will plague us—with no extra effort on their part—and impede our quest for the happiness of a loving mind.

So as a start, it is useful to investigate whether or not anger is of value. Sometimes, when we are discouraged by a difficult situation, anger does seem helpful, appearing to bring with it more energy, confidence, and determination.

Here, though, we must examine our mental state carefully. While it is true that anger brings extra energy, if we explore the nature of this energy, we discover that it is blind: we cannot be sure whether its result will be positive or negative. This is because anger eclipses the best part of our brain: its rationality. So the energy of anger is almost always unreliable. It can cause an immense amount of destructive, unfortunate behavior. Moreover, if anger increases to the extreme, one becomes like a mad person, acting in ways that are as damaging to oneself as they are to others.

It is possible, however, to develop an equally forceful but far more controlled energy with which to handle difficult situations.

This controlled energy comes not only from a compassionate attitude, but also from reason and patience. These are the most powerful antidotes to anger.

Unfortunately, many people misjudge these qualities as signs of weakness. I believe the opposite to be true: that they are the true signs of inner strength. Compassion is by nature gentle, peaceful and soft, but it is very powerful. It is those who easily lose their patience who are insecure and unstable. Thus, to me, the arousal of anger is a direct sign of weakness.

So, when a problem first arises, try to remain humble and maintain a sincere attitude and be concerned that the outcome is fair. Of course, others may try to take advantage of you, and if your remaining detached only encourages unjust aggression, adopt a strong stand. This, however, should be done with compassion, and if it is necessary to express your views and take strong countermeasures, do so without anger or ill-intent.

You should realize that even though your opponents appear to be harming you, in the end, their destructive activity will damage only themselves. In order to check your own selfish impulse to retaliate, you should recall your desire to practice compassion and assume responsibility for helping prevent the other person from suffering the consequences of his or her acts.

Thus, because the measures you employ have been calmly chosen, they will be more effective, more accurate and more forceful. Retaliation based on the blind energy of anger seldom hits the target.

Friends and Enemies

I must emphasize again that merely thinking that compassion and reason and patience are good will not be enough to develop them. We must wait for difficulties to arise and then attempt to practice them. And who creates such opportunities? Not our friends, of course, but our enemies. They are the ones who give us the most trouble. So if we truly wish to learn, we should consider enemies to be our best teacher! For a person who cherishes compassion and love, the practice of tolerance is essential, and for that, an enemy is indispensable. So we should feel grateful to our enemies, for it is they who can best help us develop a tranquil mind! Also, it is often the case in both personal and public life, that with a change in circumstances, enemies become friends.

So anger and hatred are always harmful, and unless we train our minds and work to reduce their negative force, they will continue to disturb us and disrupt our attempts to develop a calm mind. Anger and hatred are our real enemies. These are the forces we most need to confront and defeat, not the temporary "enemies" who appear intermittently throughout life.

Of course, it is natural and right that we all want friends. I often joke that if you really want to be selfish, you should be very altruistic! You should take good care of others, be concerned for their welfare, help them, serve them, make more friends, make more smiles. The result? When you yourself need help, you find plenty of helpers! If, on the other hand, you neglect the happiness of others, in the long term you will be the loser. And is friendship produced through quarrels and anger, jealousy and intense competitiveness? I do not think so. Only affection brings us genuine close friends.

In today's materialistic society, if you have money and power, you seem to have many friends. But they are not friends of yours; they are the friends of your money and power. When you lose your wealth and influence, you and I will find it very difficult to track these people down.

The trouble is that when things in the world go well for us, we become confident that we can manage by ourselves and feel we do not need friends, but as our status and health decline, we quickly realize how wrong we were. That is the moment when we learn who is really helpful and who is completely useless. So to prepare for that moment, to make genuine friends who will help us when the need arises, we ourselves must cultivate altruism!

Though sometimes people laugh when I say it, I myself always want more friends. I love smiles. Because of this I have the problem of know-ing how to make more friends and how to get more smiles, in particu-lar, genuine smiles. For there are many kinds of smiles, such as sarcastic, artificial, or diplomatic smiles. Many smiles produce no feeling of satis-faction, and sometimes they can even create suspicion or fear, can't they? But a genuine smile really gives us a feeling of freshness and is, I believe, unique to human beings. If these are the smiles we want, then we ourselves must create the reasons for them to appear.

Compassion and the World

In conclusion, I would like briefly to expand my thoughts beyond the topic of this short piece and make a wider point: individual happi-ness can contribute in a profound and effective way to the overall im-provement of our entire human community.

Because we all share an identical need for love, it is possible to feel that anybody we meet, in whatever circumstances, is a brother or sister. No matter how new the face or how different the dress and behavior, there is no significant division between us and other people. It is fool-ish to dwell on external differences, because our basic natures are the same.

Ultimately, humanity is one and this small planet is our only home. If we are to protect this home of ours, each of us needs to experience a vivid sense of universal altruism. It is only this feeling that can remove the self-centered motives that cause people to deceive and misuse one another. If you have a sincere and open heart, you naturally feel self-worth and confidence, and there is no need to be fearful of others.

I believe that at every level of society—familial, tribal, national, and international—the key to a happier and more successful world is the growth of compassion. We do not need to become religious, nor do we need to believe in an ideology. All that is necessary is for each of us to develop our good human qualities.

I try to treat whoever I meet as an old friend. This gives me a genuine feeling of happiness. It is the practice of compassion.

About His Holiness the 14th Dalai Lama

His Holiness the 14th Dalai Lama, Tenzin Gyatso, is both the head of state and the spiritual leader of Tibet. Committed to the promotion of human values such as happiness, compassion, forgiveness, tolerance, contentment and self-discipline, His Holiness travels the world speaking about the importance of such values.

Also dedicated to the promotion of religious harmony and understanding among the world's major religious traditions, His Holiness says, "All human beings are the same. We all want happiness and do not want suffering. Even people who do not believe in religion recognize the importance of these human values in making their life happier."

For more information on His Holiness the 14th Dalia Lama, visit www.dalailama.com.

Tips 21 to 40

☀ 21 Surprise Someone Today

Who in your life needs a spirit booster? Why not surprise that person today? I love the feeling that I get when I receive something unexpectedly. It doesn't have to be anything extravagant or expensive. It could be something as simple as a card or an offer to babysit for a friend.

One day I received an e-mail from my husband John. In it, he wrote a hundred words that described how much he loved me. For example, he wrote things like, "I love you, admire you, long for you, cherish you, and so forth." What a nice surprise! He made me feel loved and warmed my heart in the process. Why not do something for someone whom you love?

☀ 22 Don't Sweat the Small Stuff

Sometimes it takes my four-year-old Lia to remind me not to make a mountain out of a mole hill. Often times when Lia doesn't pick up her toys or eat her food, I will become frustrated and reprimand her. She will look at me with the cutest smile and say, "Mommy, OK!" She never fails to bring a smile to my face and remind me not to sweat the small stuff. And I do need plenty of reminders as anyone who knows me will tell you how easily I tend to get upset.

When you find yourself getting upset over the "small stuff" in your life, do what I do. Ask yourself, "What is the worst that can happen?" Your train is running late, and you're going to be late for work. You're already going to be late. Getting upset is not going to change anything. Or you planned on cooking a nice family dinner, but you just don't have time. Oh, well, today's the day you order out!

☀ 23 Take a Soothing Bath

Whenever I've had a particularly rough day, nothing de-stresses me like a warm bath. Often times, I light a candle and dim the lights in my bathroom to create more of a calming effect. I lock the door so that my husband and children know that mommy needs some time to herself.

As a writer, I can tell you that I've come up with many ideas in the bathtub. Why? Because when your body is in a relaxed state, your mind is also calm and free to roam in creativity.

☼ **24** Keep a Journal

Keep a journal and write down whatever comes to mind. If you are angry and need to get something off your chest, write down what is bothering you. If you're feeling creative and want to write a story or a poem, do it. If you're thankful for something or someone, put it in writing.

There are many reasons to put pen to paper. For one, putting things in writing will help you release any suppressed feelings. When you need a spirit booster, go back and read some of your entries. It will help you realize that things aren't as bad as they may seem and shift your focus to the many positives in your life. (See PT Journal on page 97).

☼ **25** Go on a Date

At this writing, my husband John and I have been married for over ten years, yet we still go on our occasional dates. At times, John and I become so consumed with our work and the kids that we forget about us. This can be dangerous because it can lead to feelings of neglect which, when left unaddressed, can lead to unfulfilled relationships and eventually divorce.

So spend some one-on-one time with your partner. Allot some time to focus your attention on you and your significant other. If you don't have a partner, go out with a special friend. Remember, the point is for you to clear your mind of everyday worries and just have some fun.

☼ 26 Seek Out Spirit Boosters

Optimism is definitely contagious. So if you want to nourish your spirit and be happy, you must surround yourself with spirit boosters or optimists. And by the same token, we need to separate ourselves from happiness suppressors or as, I like to call them, soul suckers and let them know that we won't tolerate their constant negativity.

These soul suckers are the ones who never have anything nice to say. They very rarely pay people a compliment, and they rather harp on your weaknesses rather than on your strong points. These are the so-called friends who more often than not bring your spirit down, not up. These are the people who bring out the worst in you; they dampen your spirit and refuse to see the positive side. Until recently, I always thought I had to put up with these people. But I know now that I have a right to be with people who make me feel good about myself. I have a right to be around the people who make me laugh and feel happy and so do you.

So seek out spirit boosters and weed out the soul suckers in your life. Surround yourself with family and friends who truly make you happy.

☼ 27 Give Someone a Hug

The truth is I love to hug and be hugged. My friends often describe me as "very touchy, feely." It's true, and I wouldn't have it any other way.

Besides the obvious feel-good benefits of hugging, studies have shown that touch is needed for both our emotional and physical well-being. In fact, researchers have found that hugging helps to lower blood pressure and boost the hormone oxytocin which is released during sexual climax in both sexes. It is also believed to aid in social bonding and trust.

☼ **28** Don't Hold Grudges . . . Forgive

The greatest injustice you can do to yourself is to refuse to forgive. People often think of forgiveness as something we give to others to release them from their guilt or wrongdoing. Many feel that forgiveness is something that is asked for and must be earned before it is given. But forgiveness means so much more. It is about self-healing not self-vindication.

It is a gift that you give not to others but to yourself. The person who has done wrong does not matter. What does matter is what is taking place inside of your mind and body. Holding onto anger and betrayal will only make matters worse. By holding on, the person you have not forgiven owns you. This is why the only person you are hurting when you choose not to forgive is yourself. Carrying around hatred and resentment is like drinking toxic poison on a daily basis.

Forgiving does not mean that you condone the act. True forgiveness is only possible when you acknowledge the wrong done by others and forgive them anyway. By doing so, you give yourself the freedom to love and be happy once again. It is impossible to love without forgiveness.

Admittedly, letting go of a difficult event in our lives can be extremely difficult. We've all grappled with the issue of forgiveness at one time or another. But to imprison ourselves in a vortex of hatred will only create more unhappiness and bitterness. Your energy is better spent moving on.

Who do you need to forgive in your life? Lewis B. Smedes said it right: "To forgive is to set a prisoner free and discover that the prisoner was you."

☼ **29** Don't Compete or Compare

It amazes me sometimes how much people feel the need to compete or compare their lives to others. This is such a waste of time and energy. I've come to realize over the years that another person's success has no bearing on me. Another person's success does not hurt me. However, if I can share his happiness, it can only help me.

We are all different. Therefore, we define success and happiness in different ways. So don't compete with your friends or compare your life to theirs. Instead, be happy for others. And I mean be truly happy. You'll be surprised how good you will feel.

☀ 30 Let Go of Yesterday

One of the things that I've noticed is that I've spent a lot of precious time living in the past. I've concentrated on many of the "not so happy" things that happened rather than enjoying the happiness of the moment. Or I have refused to see a friendship for what it really is because my heart was still stuck on the way things used to be years ago. It took me a long time to realize that living in the past was causing me to neglect the present and preventing me from being truly happy.

Look at things for what they are today and not for what they once were. Realize that both circumstances and people change. If you're in a relationship that no longer makes you happy, move on. Doing so can be very difficult, but it is the only way you will find happiness.

☀ 31 Do it NOW

Far too often in life, we know what we want, but we don't do anything about it. We tend to make up excuses like, "I don't have time or I have to take care of more important things." We tell ourselves that we will do what it takes to make ourselves happy later. Well, I have news for you! Later may never come, and no matter what else is going on, you can do what it takes to be happy right now!

When my daughters were infants, I put my writing on the back burner. I rationalized that I had no time, and besides I was a mother now and needed to give my children my undivided attention. I must confess, although I love my children to no end, I still felt like something was missing in my life. Once I made up my mind to start writing again (even if it was in the middle of the night), I found true happiness once again.

☀ **32** Take a Stroll Down Memory Lane

One of the happiest and most memorable days of my life was my wedding day. And although I can't turn back the clock and relive that day, I can certainly replay all those wonderful memories over and over again in my mind. I do this simply by watching my wedding video with my husband or flipping through the pages of our wedding album. And it doesn't matter how many times I take this familiar stroll down memory lane, I get a happiness rush every single time.

Think of some of the memories you would love to recreate. Perhaps you would like to relive some of your childhood memories by revisiting a place of your youth, such as the house you grew up in, the high school that you attended, or the favorite hangout of you and your friends.

☀ **33** Get a Massage

Anyone who's ever had a massage will tell you how wonderful and relaxing it can be (depending on the skill of your masseuse, of course.) But a massage does far more than make you feel good; it also helps your body release endorphins (the body's natural pain killers). At the same time, it can boost your immune system and reduce rigidity, pain, and stress.

There are many different types of massages available. So choose the one that you think will make you the most relaxed. Personally, I prefer a hot stone message; I find the combination of stone and heat on my body to be very therapeutic. But, again, you need to find the method that works best for you.

☀ **34** Color Your Mood

Have you ever wondered why people tend to wear black clothes to funerals or why red is often used in print advertisements? The answer is simple: color most definitely affects our mood. Black dampens mood and is known to signify mourning or sadness. Red is known as the color of passion and tends to stimulate arousal and enhance awareness.

Blue is the calming color while orange is cheery and purple comforting. There have been many studies which suggest that color can either lift your spirits or dampen them. So the next time you grab your paint brush, choose your colors carefully. Surround yourself with warm and inviting colors. And keep your vase filled with fresh orange and yellow flowers. Watch how they change your mood for the better!

☀ **35** Treat Yourself to a Makeover

Whenever I change my appearance—whether it is with a new hairstyle, clothes, new glasses, etc.—I never fail to feel better about myself. I may not always like my hair, but it still feels great knowing that I did something just for me. And when people compliment me on my new look, I feel even better. So go ahead, treat yourself to a new you!

☀ **36** Know the World Is Not a Terrible Place

During one of my recent shopping trips, I received a wonderful gift from a stranger. I was having a rough day and decided to go shopping. After I had finished my shopping and was putting my young daughter Lia in her car seat, I failed to strap her in while I was unloading my bags into the front seat. After I was finished, I closed the front door to hear my daughter screaming.

Unbeknownst to me, Lia had reached forward and got her fingers caught in the front passenger door. Once I realized this, I quickly opened the door and ran to look at my daughter's fingers. Her fingers did not appear to be broken, but I was in a panic trying to figure out what to do. At that moment a young woman came running up to me and handed me a cup of ice. I placed Lia's fingers in the ice, and she finally calmed down.

This wonderful woman saw what had happened and ran into Target to get some ice. I can't even begin to tell you how grateful I was. Not only did she do something nice for my daughter, but she reminded me that the world is not such a terrible place. Yes, I was having a bad day, but things could have been much worse.

☀ **37** Don't Take Things Personally

I have to admit I am still working hard on this one. Let's face it. Some-times, it is very difficult not to take things personally. We just can't help taking things to heart at times. But what's important to realize is that things are not always what they seem. The cashier at the local super-market may have been very rude to you yesterday, for example, but it may have had nothing at all to do with you. Perhaps, she was unhappy with her boss, and she took it out on her customers.

The next time someone is rude to you for no reason, tell yourself that it isn't you. Then brush it off and enjoy your day. You'll be surprised how much better you'll feel.

☀ **38** Have a Party for No Reason

There's nothing like the warmth of the company of our family and friends. But these days as our schedules become more and more hectic; we tend to see our loved ones only on special occasions.

I love going to parties because it is opportunity for me to get together with my large extended family. But while most people tend to get to-gether for a reason, my family and I get together for no reason at all. We have a party just so we can get together. It's a wonderful happiness booster.

☀ **39** Feed Your Body Right!

Have you ever wondered why people often say, "You are what you eat?" The reason is that not only can your diet have an effect on your physical well-being, but it can also affect your mental health. Good mental health foods include servings of fruit and vegetables and those that contain important fatty acids, such as salmon, walnuts, and bananas.

A varied diet is extremely important since no one food can give your body all the nutrients that it needs. Experts recommend that you choose the suggested amounts of servings from each of the five major food groups daily which are vegetables, fruits, whole grains, milk, and meat. If you are a vegetarian, you can get enough protein and other nutrients as long as you eat the right variety of food.

☀ **40** Create Your Own Space

I can't begin to tell you how many times I have gone to my husband, ranting and raving, telling him that I need my own space. Since I am a writer, my desk is like a sacred sanctuary to me. I tend to feel violated every time my husband or my children ruffle the papers on my desk or mix up my computer files. Each time, my husband reminds me that we have room for only one office and I'll have to make the most of it for now.

I may not have my own office, but I still need my own space. I still need to set time aside for just me. We all do. So for now, my bathtub has become my space. When I need time to myself away from my "screaming" kids, I run some warm bath water, light a candle, reach for some bath oil, and relax. No one is allowed to disturb me. This is my time to be alone with my thoughts. Try it.

Debbie Gisonni
www.reallifelessons.com

Nine Ways to Get Happy Anytime, Anywhere

IF WE BELIEVE ARISTOTLE who said, "Human happiness is so important it transcends all other worldly considerations," then we should strive to make happiness the first priority on our "to do" lists. Below are nine ways (based on the nine letters in the word "happiness") that you can bring more happiness and inner peace into everyday life.

1. H = Humor.

Don't you love being around someone who makes you laugh? Some of us can find humor in just about any situation, and some of us have to work at it. Remember practice makes perfect. The more you laugh, the more you will. Laughter helps lighten the darkest of days, and as an added bonus, studies show that it helps boost the immune system. And if you're healthier, you're naturally happier.

2. A = Acceptance.
You must always accept yourself, with all your imperfections, and accept your life with all its ups and downs. Imperfections are what make you interesting. Life's ups and downs are what make it exciting. Next time you look in the mirror, find something about you to love, no matter how small. And then the following week, move on to something bigger. Hey, you may even get to your thighs someday! Now, that's a big step for most of us women!

3. P = Peace
Peace can mean a lot of things on many levels, but most importantly, it's the peace you feel within you. If you accept and love yourself, you'll naturally be at peace inside. Peace enables you to respect others beliefs, even when they're different than your own, or walk away from arguments. Next time you're around that one relative who always pushes your buttons, don't argue with him, don't disagree . . . just let him be.

4. P = Play too!
There are twenty-four hours in a day. If you spend eighteen of them working and the remaining six sleeping, like many people do, you can't possibly be happy. Play could be spending quality time with your family. It could be a spa treatment, a hobby, a vacation, or even sex! And of course, it could also be child's play – swinging on a swing set, spinning a hula hoop around your hips, jumping on a huge trampoline like I do!

5. I = Intuition
Believe it or not, tapping into your natural insight and intuition will make life much easier and happier. Listen to that little voice inside of you—that gut feeling. It can save you lots of time thinking and agonizing over decisions, and in some cases, it may even save your life. The best way to develop your intuition is through some kind of meditative practice. That could be as simple as a brisk walk, a yoga class, or a few deep breaths.

6. N = Nurture.
You must remember to nurture all of you: the physical, emotional, and

spiritual you. On the spiritual side, this means giving yourself time to be alone and connect with your inner self to create that inner peace. On the emotional side, it means doing things that make you feel good as long as you're not harming another person—quality time with loved ones, eating chocolate (my favorite), gardening. The physical side is about taking care of your body with nutritious food and exercise.

7. E = Enjoy
In order to enjoy life, you must live in the present. We spend a lot of time thinking about what has already happened or what might happen, rather than enjoying what's happening right now. Enjoying life also means using it. Use your good china for a casual lunch; burn those candles you bought. You can't save life for later. You can't take your belongings with you when you leave. Surround yourself with things you enjoy; use them, and share them with others.

8. S = Slow Down
Let's face it. We're all in a big fat rush all the time. When we move quickly, we push aside all the things that truly give our life meaning, like being generous or thankful or nice to people. At the end of your life, it doesn't matter how much you got done in record time. What matters is how many connections you made with people; how much love you gave, and how much thanks you had.

9. S = Surrender
We are so hard-wired to control—to make things happen with our will. What's important to remember about surrendering is that it's not about giving up—it's about trusting. Surrendering doesn't mean giving up your power, but rather empowering your spirit within you to take over the controls once in a while. It means going with the flow, even though you don't know where it's taking you. It means accepting that things happen when and if they should.

If you practice these nine tips, you will definitely be happier, but *only* if you believe it and feel it. In *The Goddess of Happiness* book, I have an affirmation at the end of each chapter. Above the affirmation are the words: "Think it! Say it! Feel it!" To create anything in your life, you must imagine how it feels and really believe it. Your thoughts and emotions have tremendous power in affecting your body, your environment, and your reality.

About Debbie Gisonni

Debbie Gisonni is a best-selling author, speaker, happiness expert, columnist, and former corporate executive. At the height of her executive career, her life was derailed when she lost four family members in just four years. At this difficult time, she realized she wasn't the Queen Bee she once thought she was. Rather, she was an ordinary Goddess with the power to be happy, no matter what.

She left her corporate career to start her own company (Real Life Lessons) to help people navigate the ups and downs of everyday life from the ecstatic to the tragic and everything in between. Her mission is to make life easier and happier whether that means helping someone follow a dream or just sharing a simple pasta dish.

For more information about Debbie, please visit her website at www.reallifelessons.com or contact her at debbieg@reallifelessons.com.

Tips 41 to 60

☀ **41** Relax with a Drink

Recent studies have found that drinking red wine in moderation can actually improve your health. Well, I must admit that I love red wine and couldn't have been happier when I heard about research which indicated that it could actually lower cholesterol levels and protect against certain cancers. My parents are from Italy, and red wine has always been a staple on the dinner table.

But I love red wine for another reason as well: it helps me relax. I love to savor the taste and drink slowly as I notice the texture of the wine in my mouth. I am not suggesting that you become intoxicated, however. One glass is said to be the moderate limit for woman and two for men.

If you can't drink alcohol, drink whatever satisfies your palate whether it is coffee, juice, soda, etc. The important thing is that you really enjoy both the drink and the moment.

☀ **42** Realize Beauty is Skin Deep

Whenever I meet someone new, it takes me a little while before I can say that I consider that person handsome or beautiful. Sure I feel an instant physical attraction to some people. But the truth is that initial physical attraction is second to my attraction to someone on the inside. To me, you are not truly beautiful unless you are beautiful on the inside.

Because of this, I find myself taking more time to get to know people, and as a result, I get a sense of who they really are. It helps me form more meaningful, lasting relationships. So when you meet someone new, try to look at him from the inside out instead of the outside in.

☼ **43** Listen to the Birds Sing

I have severe bilateral nerve deafness and cannot hear high-pitched sounds. Since I wasn't diagnosed until I was fourteen-years-old, I could never understand why I couldn't hear the birds sing when I was growing up. I can remember sitting on my porch looking up at the birds in the tree thinking all the birds must be sleeping.

Today, I still wish I could hear the birds sing, but it doesn't bother me nearly as much as it did when I was younger. Nowadays, the birds are a constant reminder to me not to take life for granted. They are a constant sign to me that life is much too short.

As you go about your day, cherish all of it. Remember not to take anything for granted and take time to listen to the birds sing.

☼ **44** Don't Be a Complainer

To those of you who know me, yes, I do recognize myself loudly and clearly in this one. I have definitely done my share of complaining. Luckily, though, I have realized that complaining only makes things worse.

Think of it this way: each time you complain, it is impossible to even think about the positive side of any situation. Instead, we focus on negativity and not ways to make things better. What's more, we bring others down with us. And we all know that no one likes to be around someone who is constantly complaining. So take note of how often you are complaining. It's the first step to changing your behavior.

☼ **45** Get Enough Sleep

Of course, getting enough shuteye not only helps to restore physical energy, but it is also extremely important for our emotional well-being. When people are tired due to lack of sleep, it can affect the way they respond to day–to–day situations. For example, simple problems may make them irritable and temperamental. And as a result, they are less likely to think positively and tend to be more miserable.

Generally, our bodies need seven to ten hours of sleep a night. Doing so ensures that our bodies get enough sleep to boost our immune system, to improve our cognitive motor skills, and to look as well as feel better all the way around. When we don't get enough sleep, we may experience sickness, poor work performance, and irritability among other things.

But everyone is different, and only you can pinpoint how many hours of sleep your body actually needs. Once you have determined the appropriate number, try to stick to a regular sleep schedule. For example, get up and go to bed at the same time every day. Also, avoid alcohol or caffeine late in the day, and do something to help yourself relax before you go to bed. You may want to try taking a warm bath, listening to soft music, or reading a book. If nothing seems to help, seek the help of your physician.

☀ 46 Go Out to Eat

I love making breakfast, lunch, and dinner for my family. But once in a while, I just need to get out. During the weekend, I enjoy going to my favorite local diner and ordering a big, healthy breakfast. Or there are just some days when I need a break in my routine and seek out a new hot spot for lunch or dinner. I enjoy the diversion of going someplace different and find pleasure in knowing that there are no dirty dishes for me to clean up.

So go ahead and try that new restaurant that just opened up in town. Or treat yourself to breakfast tomorrow morning. Just the thought of knowing that you'll be going out to eat will bring you pleasure.

☀ **47** Watch Your Thoughts

As a little girl growing up with a disability, I often felt sorry for myself.
I resented the fact that I couldn't do many of the things most of my
classmates took for granted every day. For example, since I had terrible
balance, I was never able to ice skate, ski, or even ride a skate board. But
as I got older, I realized that I was spending too much time focusing on
the things that I couldn't do and therefore ignored all the things that I
was very capable of doing. For example, I was not athletic, but I was a
good dancer. I was also very creative which allowed me to write poetry,
short stories, and the like.

As they say, you can either look at the glass as half empty or half full.
Once I made up my mind to do the latter, I no longer felt sorry for
myself and I no longer allowed others to dampen my spirit. I knew that
I had a lot to be grateful for in life, and that's all that mattered.

So watch your thoughts. Whenever your mind starts to shift into
negativity, think of something positive.

☀ **48** Spend Quality Time with Family

I've often heard people comment about how much "Italians love to eat."
But personally, I don't think Italians love the food as much as they
value spending time with family and friends. As I write this, I am warmly
reminded of my wonderful Uncle Tony. He always took great joy in
having his family and friends over his house. Whenever I would visit,
he never knew what to offer me first. I had to have a glass of his homemade wine or some *sopprasata* (dried Italian sausage) or some cheese.

Even when my Uncle Tony was dying from a tumor in his brain,
he continued to relish in the joy of spending time with his family
and friends. When he was at his worst, I used to feel guilty sitting in
the kitchen with my cousins while my uncle lay helpless in his bed.
But then one day when he could no longer eat and I stood beside
him holding his hand, I realized that this was exactly how my uncle
wanted it. He didn't care about the food; he cared only about having

his family close to him.

His death taught me a priceless lesson about the importance of spending time with family and friends. I realized how happy he was around his family and how happy I was just spending time with him. Thoughts of him always bring a smile to my face. Try to enjoy every minute of the time that you spend with your family and friends. I know I do.

☀ **49** Get to Know Someone Better

At this writing, my husband and I have known each other for twelve years. And I can honestly say that I know him better than I do any other human being. But the truth is we are still learning different things about each other. Just yesterday, for instance, John told me that he never liked white bread. I was shocked to hear this since I have been buying white bread for years.

The point, however, is not the white bread, but the fact that I continue to learn new things about John. And the more I learn about him, the closer I feel to him. It is very easy to get so tied up in our everyday lives and relationships that we tend to lose that special connection we often share with those we hold close.

When was the last time you got to know someone better, whether it is a spouse, lover, family member, or friend? Why not invite that special someone over for a cup of coffee and ask him to share something new with you.

☀ **50** Take Your Vitamins

Unfortunately, most Americans do not get enough daily vitamins and minerals. And those who do take vitamins do so without really understanding why it is so important. Vitamin B3, also called niacin, is important for converting calories into energy. Vitamin C, also called ascorbic acid, helps our immune system while Vitamin E is believed to be a powerful antioxidant.

You can, of course, derive many essential vitamins from the food you eat. So drink your milk and load up on your veggies and lima beans. Both your body and your mind will notice the difference it makes!

☀ 51 Say I'm Sorry

There is nothing heavier for the heart to carry than guilt. Many of us walk around with unnecessary negative energy because we find it difficult or even impossible to say two simple words. Yet saying "I'm sorry" is one of the biggest spirit lifters on the planet.

When you know you're wrong, why walk around with guilt? Just say you're sorry and say it like you really mean it. Not only will you make the recipient happy, but you will also feel much happier as well.

☀ 52 Plant a Garden

We all know how a garden can enhance the beauty and elegance of any home. But what many don't realize is that a garden can bring many physical and psychological rewards as well. Many who work outdoors in the garden experience a renewed sense of well-being and a boost of confidence. Others retreat to a garden for relaxation and a feeling of peace.

In addition to all the therapeutic rewards gardening can bring, taking care of flowers or a lawn has been found to increase muscle strength and flexibility, lower the risk of osteoporosis, and decrease the chances of heart disease. So get out your gardening tools; start planting your garden today!

☀ 53 Send a Note of Praise

After publishing my first book, *Footprints in the Sand: A Disabled Woman's*

Inspiring Journey to Happiness, I received an e-mail from a wonderful man named Charles. He wrote,

"I am typing this on my computer with my tongue and am one of few cerebral palsy citizens this severe who fought to have 24 hour, 7 days a week care at home—an accomplishment I am very proud of. My parents are no longer alive, but they helped me to become independent. Thank you for the book; and I hope there will be more sequels."

I couldn't ask for a better spirit booster than that. Just the fact that Charles would take the time to write me was instantly uplifting. Think about the people in your life who need a little lift. Then send them some praise with a phone call, an e-mail, or a note.

Just the act of sending someone else praise will make you feel good. I just love the feeling I get when I praise someone else; it makes my day. You may wonder why I'm the one feeling good when I'm giving the praise rather than receiving it. Well, their positive energy reflects back on you. It's a win–win situation.

When you take the time to lift someone else's spirit, you will, in turn, lift your own.

☀ **54** Live Your Own Life

When was the last time you did what you really wanted to do? It is a fact that so many of us are so busy making other people happy we neglect our own happiness. For example, you have been looking forward to a skiing trip all year, but then your parents decide to have a family reunion that same week. You talk to your mother and tell her about your trip, but she insists it would be wrong not to attend the reunion. You feel guilty so you cancel your trip. Sound familiar?

We often do things we don't want to do out of guilt. But in the end, we still feel terrible. Take charge of your life and learn how to say, "No."

☀ 55 Take in Some Warm Sun

As a skin cancer survivor, I am by no means suggesting that you sunbathe. What I am saying, however, is that fresh air and a limited amount of sun are energy boosters. Not only does the sun help our skin produce Vitamin D, but it can also be both mentally and physically revitalizing.

In fact, many people who do not get enough sun during the winter months often experience cabin fever or seasonal affective disorder (SAD). Those who have this condition often experience the feeling of depression, loneliness, and lethargy. Instead of walking on the treadmill, take a stroll outside. You'll feel the difference a little fresh air can make.

☀ 56 Watch What You Say

How many times have you said things you really didn't mean? You know the scenario. You have an argument with someone. He or she says something to make you feel bad. You retaliate with a few negative words. But after it's all said and done, it's a no-win situation. Both parties walk away feeling terrible; all of this could be avoided if you follow one rule: think before you speak.

I'll admit it's not always easier to do. But I promise you, thinking about the situation for just ten seconds will make a world of a difference.

☀ 57 Do a Reality Check

We all need a reality check every now and then. We need to take inventory of our past and present lives. When things are not going our way, we tend to think the world is out to get us. Life is so unfair. I know how it feels; the truth is I've been there many times.

But I've also learned to sit back and realize that things are never as bad as my mind sometimes makes them out to be. When I take the time to think about the reality of the situation, I see that the good in my life outweighs the bad things. I take note of the fact that I am surrounded by friends and family who love me. I then go on to mentally list all the things that I have to be grateful for—a practice that always makes me feel better.

☀ 58 Bask in Nudity

When I say nudity, I don't mean this in an erotic sense but a spiritual one. We all have issues with our physical appearance. You may not like your hair or your current weight, for example. But the truth is you need to learn to accept yourself and who you truly are. I, for one, have many scars on my body from various surgeries as a result of my skin cancer and cerebral palsy. I also have a birthmark on my right hand that looks like a brown crescent moon. I spent years regretting each time I was forced to look at my nude body in a mirror because the image didn't look exactly like the beautiful woman on those magazine covers. Unfortunately, all these "so-called" perfect bodies lead us to believe that our bodies are ugly or inadequate.

It took me a long time to realize that my body is just the house my soul lives in. In other words, my body is not what makes me beautiful or desirable but rather the person that I am deep within. Once you can feel good about that person on the inside, you'll learn to love the body on the outside.

☀ 59 Cherish What You Have

Sometimes we can get so caught up in what we want and what we think we need that we forget to appreciate what we already have.

When I first moved into my house, I spent a great deal of time focusing on all the things that my new home didn't have. For instance, I wanted four bedrooms; it has three. I had hoped for a bigger kitchen but didn't get it. The list goes on. The point is I spent so much time griping about the things I didn't have that I never took the time to appreciate all the wonderful things that I do have in my life.

The truth is I really didn't need a four bedroom house; I just wanted one. I finally realized that I was extremely fortunate. I have a wonderful husband and two beautiful children. I am surrounded by friends and family who care about me. These are the things that I truly need in my life, not material things.

So be thankful for what you have. Know that there is a big difference between your wants and needs. You will appreciate your life like you never have before.

☀ **60** Realize that You are Evolving

We are all constantly changing. Our souls are constantly searching and longing to find new meaning and understanding as we seek happiness in our lives. When we change, however, so do our relationships.

When a relationship with an old friend turned sour, I felt both upset and relieved. I was upset because we had been friends for a very long time and relieved because I realized that I wasn't the same person that I had been years earlier. I still cared about her deeply, but I didn't enjoy her company as I once did. I spent a long time feeling guilty about my emotions until I realized that I was simply evolving.

I have reached a new level of self-awareness and personal growth. I am proud of the me that I have become and look forward to the me that is still yet to come.

Geri Jewell

www.gerijewell.com

The Many Facets of Jewell

BEING BORN GERI JEWELL, I was a diamond in the rough. I came into the world with many challenges and had the tools to face them. I was diagnosed with cerebral palsy at eighteen-months-old, and from all appearances it looked as though the cerebral palsy being branded onto my hide was something of a tragic nature, but appearances can very often be deceiving. At fifty-three, I have come to believe that the cerebral palsy was a blessing in disguise.

When I was about six-years-old, my physician made the comment to my parents that I was truly one of the most content and happiest of children with a disability that he had ever encountered. He wanted to know what the secret was so that we could bottle it and make a fortune.

I believe that from early on, humor has played a key role in my development. My whole family, for the most part, laughed often. When we are laughing, we are also "healing" our pain. If we cannot laugh at ourselves, we end up being very bitter and resentful. If there is not

51

enough humor in a household, that living situation eventually will break down from the weight of all the drama.

The truth is I learned "happiness" long before I was able to conceptualize "unhappiness." Oh sure, there were always the "unpleasant, discomforting times" but because my home base was "happy," I was able to recover quickly and not allow the very real "pain" to consume me.

I spent the first three months of my life in an incubator, with no human contact. Nurses were not allowed to touch me without masks or gloves. To even begin to imagine the magnitude of coming into the world and being so isolated is difficult, but it is absolutely daunting to even think about the "loneliness." However, I lived and got stronger day after day, month after month. How?

Another "facet of Jewell" is our spiritual life, and how much we choose to become aware of it and embrace it. I believe that even though it appeared to be a "lonely" experience to be encased in a glass box for three months, the truth is, there weren't a whole lot of "distractions" to interfere with my spiritual connection. Also, I have always believed in angels! I truly believe that there were many angels who came to visit me while I was roasting in my incubator.

I also suspect that many of these "spirit guides" had a marvelous sense of humor! They probably said some jokes about how funny that I have a similar life experience as a baby chick, or along the lines, at least you have a room with a view! The point is, even though I was a preemie and wasn't expected to live by "medical" standards, life was happening!

Notice the phrase "life is happening"; the word happening in itself suggests happiness! So, no matter what "happens" in life, try to return always to that very precious spiritual beginning and not lose focus of the "precious jewels" we all are! Our purpose and passions will carry us, and our sense of humor will "lighten" the way.

Another very important "facet of Jewell" is to believe in yourself, no matter what! Throughout life people are not going to believe in us. This can be devastating, especially to those who depend on the belief of others to define how they feel about themselves. Try not to look outside yourself to build your self–esteem. The reason the word "self-esteem" begins with the word "self" is because to truly experience great self-esteem, one must look at oneself. Go within to seek the positive.

And the last, but not least "facet of Jewell" is to always live and seek truth. Hypocrisy is the most self-destructive and "disabling" thing any of us can do to ourselves. Even if the "truth" hurts, allow yourself to feel the pain, and then let it go. Walk your talk, and be honest with yourself and others.

Just the mere act of not being able to forgive the shortcomings and transgressions of others, is an act of hypocrisy. Why? Because it is hypocritical of our own desire to be forgiven. We must always forgive ourselves, and then from there, forgive others. Forgiveness is the grandest healing condition in attaining a "happening life."

So, there it is, a "few" of the "many facets of Jewell." Laugh often, stay spiritually connected, believe in yourself no matter what, and be honest always, even if the truth hurts. Remember we all are "precious jewels" and are invaluable in having the ability to make a difference in the world. In life, what matters most is what we leave in our wake. So, wake up! Live life to its fullest, and never underestimate the power of the human spirit. Namaste.

About Geri Jewell

Geri Jewell, the first person with a disability to appear regularly on a prime time series, is best known for her role as Cousin Geri on the NBC sitcom, *The Facts of Life*. She began her career as a standup comedian using humor to captivate the hearts of millions while also instilling hope among the disabled community.

After her groundbreaking role on NBC, she went on to appear on the Emmy award winning movie, *Two of a Kind, 21 Jump Street, The Young and the Restless,* the HBO hit series *Deadwood,* and many others. The recipient of several awards, Geri has been featured on *Entertainment Tonight, E Hollywood True Story,* and *ABC's 20/20.* When not working in television, she is a much sought-after motivational speaker famous for her ability to inspire others though the power of laughter.

For more information about Geri, please visit her website at www.gerijewell.com.

Tips 61 to 80

☀ **61** Give and You Shall Receive

I love to give gifts for no reason at all. My friends usually look at me smiling and say, "What did you do that for?" Honestly, I like to give gifts because it makes me feel good. The smile that I elicit from the recipient makes me feel warm all over.

But I must warn you. You cannot give to others with the intent of getting something back in return. You will end up disappointed if you don't get what you are looking for.

Do something simply to make someone else happy. It could be as simple as giving up your seat on the train during your morning commute. When you make others happy, you will experience happiness in return.

☀ **62** Take a Yoga Class

Though yoga is believed to be over four–thousand–years–old, it continues to be an increasingly popular form of exercise as more and more people recognize the benefits of uniting the mind, body, and spirit.

By combining body position and breathing techniques, participants are able to achieve a state of mind that has proven to bring both mental and physical benefits. Yoga, for example, helps to decrease anxiety, depression, and stress while also increasing flexibility and muscle tone. Doing so allows for good blood flow through the body which helps to flush out bad toxins and lessen the signs of aging.

If you'd prefer to try yoga in the comfort of your own home, I'd recommend you pick up a book by Dawn Groves entitled *Yoga for Busy People*. Dawn describes many yoga exercises that can be easily done at home. My favorite is The Standing Chair Hang—a quick way to stretch your lower back after a long day at your desk. Here are the steps:

Get a stable chair and stand about three feet behind it. Now, grab the back of the chair with your hands keeping them about twelve inches apart.

Bend forward at the hips keeping your arms and legs straight. Make sure your hips and thighs are moving away from your hands. Relax. Inhale. Exhale.

To finish, step toward the chair, release the chair back and slowly roll up, one vertebra at a time.

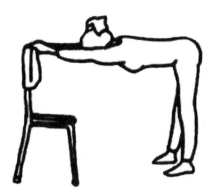

Though it may take a while in the beginning to fully relax and restore positive energy through the various yoga techniques, practice makes perfect. Before long, you will begin to find yourself feeling undeniably invigorated and rested.

☀ **63** Don't Take People for Granted

After ten years of marriage, my husband still thanks me for dinner every time I give him a home-cooked meal. I can make hamburgers on the grill, and he will still thank me. I love him for it. His simple words of gratitude make me feel appreciated and not taken for granted.

Too often, acts of kindness go unnoticed. When someone does something nice, let him know that you appreciate it.

☀ **64** Reach Out to an Old Friend

As we get older and more involved with our children, careers, and lives, it sometimes becomes difficult to stay in touch with our old friends. But the truth is while our new friends know the people we have become, our old friends know us as we have always been.

My friend Adriana and I have been friends since I was about twelve years old. We don't see each other often, but when we do, it's as if no time has passed. We sometimes talk on the phone for hours just strolling down memory lane as we attempt to recapture our youth.

It is always a pleasant surprise to pick up the phone and hear Adriana's comforting, familiar voice on the other end. She always brings a smile to my face. So if you haven't spoken to an old friend in a while, pick up the phone. You will make her day as well as your own.

☀ **65** Please Yourself First

I have to admit I am a people pleaser. I want things to be perfect all the time and everybody to be happy. But I've learned a hard lesson over the years. It is impossible to please everyone and what's more, it's not worth the effort. Why? Because when you spend so much time running around trying to satisfy everyone else, most of the time, you end up dissatisfying yourself. You do things not because you want to, but because you think it's the right thing to do.

You habitually give in to others because you can't stand the thought of upsetting them. So you push your needs aside for the benefit of others. And in the process, you end up unhappy. I'm not saying that you should never please others, but what I am saying is that you are first and foremost. You are the first person that you have to please. Everyone else is second. Try putting yourself first once in a while.

☀ **66** Start Anew . . . It's Never Too Late

I once read about a woman who decided to realize her dreams and became a doctor at the age of sixty. Some people might think of this as crazy. She is, after all, close to retirement age. But I'm not one of those people. I think it's amazing, and I admire this woman for her unyielding spirit.

It didn't matter how old she was. Whether she went to medical school or not, she was still eventually going to turn sixty. That's the part that we all can't change, our age. But we can control how we age. We do have power over how we live our life and how we choose to seek happiness in it.

At this writing, I am a mother, author, speaker, and inventor. But there are still so many more things that I'd like to do. And I plan on trying every single one.

☀ **67** Get a Physical

We've already talked about the many benefits of exercise. But taking care of yourself and your body entails much more than getting exercise and taking vitamins. It means eating healthy, sleeping well, and getting regular physicals. Yes, I mean going to see a doctor once in a while.

I hate going to the doctor, but I go as often as my body needs to. I feel a sense of relief after I've had an exam and my doctor tells me everything is alright. I feel better both emotionally and physically. So take care of yourself; you'll notice how good you feel!

☀ **68** Look Into Their Eyes

Eyes are said to tell the secrets of the heart. How we look at someone, whether it is with a nervous glance or a deep gaze, reveals how we feel about him or the situation. It is also the most crucial part of making a positive first impression.

Making eye contact with someone lets him know, for instance, that you are interested in him or that you are being honest. Looking away or refusing to look someone in the eyes can mean that you are nervous, arrogant, or dishonest.

☀ 69 Concentrate on Something Beautiful

Whenever I need a pick-me-up, I look at my two daughters. To me, both of them are beautiful and were conceived from an unyielding love between me and my husband. I get a happiness rush every time I look at them. Sometimes they even bring tears to my eyes as I am reminded time and time again of just how lucky I really am.

So feast your eyes on something beautiful. You'll find it impossible not to smile and, as a result, will feel good all over.

☀ 70 Stop Blaming Others

We are all experts at the "blame game." We say things like, "It wasn't my fault; you're the one who started it; it's because of you," etc. We are so quick to blame others rather than face up to the situation and realize our mistakes.

Stop blaming others. Take responsibility for your actions and recognize your faults. You'll be the better person for it.

☀ 71 Smile a Lot

Over the years, much has been said of how many muscles in the human body are used to smile and to frown. Scientists have said it takes forty-one muscles to frown but only sixteen muscles to smile. Although the required number of needed muscles seems to change with each telling, the fact that it is much easier to smile than frown remains the same.

Those who smile more tend to be more optimistic and those who are optimistic tend to live healthier, happier lives. Think about it. Have you ever been able to smile and be angry at the same time? Once in the middle of an argument with my husband, I decided to smile. Doing so made me laugh, and I found myself forgetting what we were even arguing about in the first place.

Smiling is also contagious. The more you smile, the happier you will make others.

☀ 72 Buy Yourself Some Flowers

Flowers are instant mood elevators. So go out and buy yourself some flowers for no reason at all. I pick up flowers every week at my local grocery store. The flowers need not be expensive or extravagant. Just go out and buy whatever will make you feel good! You deserve it!

☀ 73 Allow Yourself to be Happy

Far too often, we do not allow ourselves to be happy. We do this in numerous ways. For instance, we live in the past instead of letting go and concentrating on the present. We downplay the good things that happen to us while accentuating the bad things.

When someone asks you how you're doing, how many times have you said, "OK," when you really felt like saying, "Great?" How many times have you refrained from telling someone about your raise or promotion at work because you didn't want to seem like you were bragging?

☀ 74 Sing a Song

I may not have a good singing voice, but as my husband and kids will tell you that doesn't stop me from starting up a tune or two around the house. I love to sing because it makes me feel good. It helps to release all the emotion that I sometimes keep bottled up inside.

The truth is that half the time I don't even know the words to the songs. So I end up making them up. I'm sure both the song and my voice are less than perfect. But I don't care. It's fun, and I sing for me and no one else.

☀ 75 Learn from Your Mistakes

We all make mistakes and that's OK. They are an important part of life. But the worst thing that can happen is when you don't learn anything from them. Try to think of mistakes as an opportunity because they allow you to see where you need to improve.

To grow, you need to learn and to learn you need to make some mistakes. If you can see mistakes in a new light, then you won't be so hard on yourself when you do make them.

☀ 76 Say How You Feel

So many of us hold back from telling those close to us how we really feel simply because of fear. We are so afraid we are not going to get the response we want that we resort to keeping our thoughts inside.

The longer we hold our feelings inside, the harder it is to let them out. As a result, our emotions continue to build up until we finally release them. Only now the probability of doing so in a rational manor is about nil.

So even though it may seem easier to keep quiet in the beginning, the situation will likely only get worse in the end. The only solution is to say what is truly on your mind, and say it soon.

☀ 77 Realize You Create Your Own Destiny

Simply stated, according to metaphysical law, what we believe is and what we don't believe isn't. If you truly believe that you can achieve something, then you will take steps to achieve it and most likely will succeed. If, however, you don't believe it, you will fail.

Everything happens for a reason. You're where you are now and going where you're going in the future because of your actions and beliefs right now. Even though we sometimes feel like we have no control over what happens, the truth is we do have power over what happens to us.

We are in control of our own destiny.

☀ 78 Use Verbal Affirmations

The first time I was asked to speak before a large group, I can remember feeling very anxious. I e-mailed my friend Sue, a motivational speaker and author, telling her how I felt. She quickly replied telling me not to tell anyone that I was nervous. She said it was very important to keep saying "I'm looking forward to it."

So during the month before the big day, I kept telling myself and anyone who asked that I was looking forward to my presentation. And when it was finally time to speak, I actually was looking forward to it. I didn't feel nervous anymore because I was there to share my experiences and to help others.

Sue was basically encouraging me to use verbal affirmations in order to stay positive and to believe in myself. Affirmations are positive statements or words that can either be spoken or written. By repeating these affirmations over and over, you will eventually believe what you are saying. The important thing to remember, however, is that these affirmations will do little to change your attitude unless you truly feel what you are saying or writing.

If I kept telling myself that my speech was going to help others but yet I did nothing to try and help others, my affirmations would be fruitless. Or perhaps I was just speaking out of obligation and in my heart of hearts really didn't want to. If that were the case, then all the affirmations in the world wouldn't make a difference.

If you think you can, you can and you will. As Henry Ford once said, "Whether you think you can or you think you can't, either way, you are correct."

☀ 79 Get Away for a While

A surprising number of Americans do not use all of their vacation time each year, and when they are off from work, many still check in with the office. This may be happy news to many employers, but the fact of the matter is that it's the employees who suffer. Studies have shown, for example, that those who forgo taking vacations for long periods of time are more likely to suffer from heart disease.

If you just can't take that much-needed vacation, then just take the day off for no reason. Change your scenery and get away for a while. To me, there is no better place to recharge my energy than the beach. I love the sound of the recurrent ocean and the feel of the sand beneath me. And if I want to just unwind and have fun, I enjoy a trip to New York City with my husband. Since we live in New Jersey, I can enjoy the excitement of the City without being too far away from my children.

☀ 80 Decorate Your Home

Just as it is a good spirit booster to change your daily routine, it is just as important to change the scenery in the place where you spend the most time: your home.

You need not spend a lot of money to decorate or improve your home. If you choose, you may want to purchase a new piece of furniture or redo your landscaping. But you can also do simple things like put up a new picture in your bedroom, change the knobs and hinges on your cabinets in the kitchen, or buy a new table lamp for your living room.

Sue Hershkowitz-Coore

www.SpeakerSue.com

Accentuate the Positive

I'VE NEVER SPENT MUCH time thinking about what happiness is. From the time I was very young, my parents didn't accept negative thinking. I was just raised to be happy with my lot, and if I wasn't, then it was my choice—and responsibility—to do something about it.

If my brother or I complained about something—anything—they'd always have a more positive way of looking at it. For instance, if I complained about being cold while we were out, my dad would say, "What are you going to do in the wintertime?" Mind you, it *was* wintertime, and freezing! When I'd remind my dad of that fact, he'd act like he had never thought of that, laugh and say, "Then think about the summertime." Or, if I fell and scraped my knee and cried, he'd pick me up and say, "I hope you didn't crack the sidewalk, let's see, oh you did, oh the poor sidewalk!"

I'd be furious at him, but in all the attention the sidewalk was getting, I'd stop crying! Or, if I'd whine about having to eat my mother's vegetable choice—canned string beans—she'd say, "There are starving children in China; you're lucky to have food, eat." Of course, none of these "wise" sayings made me very happy then, but in thinking about it, they taught me to always see the positive side of the situation, not to feel sorry for myself, work hard, and just keep going.

When my first boyfriend broke up with me and I moped around the house, my mother handed me a copy of Norman Vincent Peale's book, *The Power of Positive Thinking.* And we're Jewish! Dr. Peale had it right and so did Bing Crosby who sang, "Accentuate the Positive." (Written by Johnny Mercer/Harold Arlen) My dad played that song on "78" speed, and I knew every word. It just spoke to who we were and how we were being taught to look at life.

I have always tried to handle my life in that positive (but odd) way. After my son was in a terrible motorcycle accident, he required a great deal of orthopedic surgery. His wrist has never stopped hurting him. When he complains, I say, "That's to remind you of how lucky you are to be alive." (His reply, "Oh, you're such a motivational speaker!")

What exactly is happiness? To me, being happy is feeling content with what you have or doing something different. It's the old how can I make lemonade out of these lemons type thinking. We all have lemons, some of us are handed quite a few of them, but what's the choice? Wallow in pity and keep being sour or working hard to find some sugar to mix in? Knowing that I can impact my own destiny by continuing to emphasize the positive is what makes me happiest. And that's what I try to teach others.

About Sue Hershkowitz-Coore

An internationally recognized speaker and communications expert, Sue helps audiences increase their professionalism and productivity through improved communications skills. She has spoken before more than a million people worldwide and authored such books as *Power Sales Writing* and *How to Say It to Sell It!* and has been quoted in *USA Today, CEO Insights, Entrepreneur,* and *Selling Power.*

A member of the National Speakers Association and a founding member of Meeting Professional International's Women's Leadership Initiative, Sue uses her contagious enthusiasm to help others think outside the box and to achieve greater results, both professionally and personally.

For more information about Sue, please visit www.SpeakerSue.com or contact her at Sue@SpeakerSue.com.

Tips 81 to 105

☀ **81** Release Your Anger

We all experience anger, and we are allowed to be angry. The difference, though, is that some people are able to release feelings of anger and blame after a short period of time while others tend to harbor these feelings deep inside for a long time.

When we are angry, we naturally attract more anger which hurts us both physically and emotionally. Physically anger leads to sickness, and emotionally it can cause us to detach ourselves from family and friends. Anger keeps us from truly forgiving someone and thus keeps us from giving and receiving love.

I admit that I am a very emotional person. When I love someone, I let him know. And when I'm angry, I can't hide it. It shows all over my face. But what I do is allow myself to be angry for a period of time and that's it. I don't dwell in anger because when you're angry, you are allowing your spirit to be taken over by negativity.

I said it before and I'll say it again and again, life is too short to be spent focusing on the bad. So go ahead and write your feelings on a piece of paper, yell, scream. Do whatever you need to do to release the anger (without hurting anyone else, of course). You'll feel much better and attract harmony back into your life.

☀ **82** Know When it's Time to Let Go

How many times have you stayed in a relationship despite your unhappiness? You've been friends with someone for a very long time. And although you know that you no longer have anything in common and don't enjoy each other's company, you remain "so-called" friends. Or your spouse continues to put you down and you don't like the way you're being treated. Yet you continue to stay in the abusive relationship.

There's no easy way to cope when this happens. But you need to know when enough is enough and make up your mind to let go. Move on and find the happiness that you deserve.

☀ 83 Surround Yourself with Memories

In my living room, two very special photos of lighthouses adorn my walls. These pictures were taken during a trip to Cape Cod, Massachusetts, when my husband proposed. In my bedroom, a beautiful pinkish–colored seashell sits on top of my television. I cherish it because I found it while strolling on the beach in Antigua.

Many more memories adorn the walls or sit on shelves in my home. Each one takes me back to a very particular time in my life. Each one fills me with warmth and gratitude.

☀ 84 Set Goals for Yourself

Think about what you want to achieve in life and then write down your goals. Doing so will give you a sense of purpose and direction. Also having a written list of goals will help you to stay focused and to channel your time and energy toward reaching each one.

These can be long–term or short–term goals. Where do you want to be in five years? Maybe, you want to write a book or get a graduate degree.

There are some rules, however. You have to have a plan; you must want to succeed; the goals must be reasonable, and you must truly believe you can achieve them.

☀ 85 Wake Up with a Positive Thought

If you're like most people, you wake up thinking about all the endless things you have to do for the day. Chances are you are worried that you have too much to do and not enough time to do them all. These negative thoughts make you tense before you even start your day. These thoughts also set the tone for the rest of your day.

Try this. When you wake up, don't rush out of bed (if you don't have to). Relax for one minute and think about something positive. It's a beautiful day for the beach or maybe you're looking forward to a date with your mate or spending time with your children. Think about something or someone that makes you happy.

☀ **86** Listen to Music

Music is a great way to nourish your spirit. Different types of songs affect people in different ways. For me, listening to *Ave Maria* does the trick. When my spirit needs a lift, I sometimes close my eyes and sit in a quiet place while this song plays in the background. It seems to have a mystical effect on me as my mind rids itself of all negative thoughts and replaces them with calming, encouraging ones.

Doctors and therapist use music in a variety of ways including to lower blood pressure, to treat depression, and even to treat Attention Deficit Disorder in children. It is not the words in the song but the tune that creates the healing effects.

Find out which music works for you.

☀ **87** Hire Someone to Help Out

There is nothing that I dislike more than a messy house, but I find myself letting things go more and more now as I juggle the responsibilities of being a mother, wife, and writer. So whenever possible, I hire someone to give my house that "top to bottom" clean.

It gives me such a sense of relief knowing that my house will be taken care of and realizing that I can then attend to other things which I consider more important such as spending more time with my children.

So whether it's to clean your house or mow your lawn, hiring someone may bring the ease and comfort your mind and body need.

☀ **88** Go for a Walk

Out of all the physical activities available, none perhaps have more benefits than walking. In fact, there are too many to list. A daily walk can help to keep your weight under control, reduce the risk of having a heart attack, stroke, diabetes, high blood pressure, or osteoporosis, and even gives you more energy.

But besides the above benefits, walking just makes you feel good. It helps you to relax and think more clearly. It doesn't matter how little or how long you walk, every bit helps.

☀ **89** Break Your Normal Routine

Sometimes I feel like my life is on autopilot. My mind seems to be saying: make the kids breakfast, get them to school, come home and do the laundry, work on the book, pick up the kids, cook dinner, etc. How many times have you felt like you were in a rut?

Sometimes a simple solution is to just break your routine. How do you break your routine? Simply do something a little different. Take a trip to someplace you've never been before. It doesn't have to be far away. Get in the car and drive to a neighborhood in your hometown that you've never seen before. Consider something new for dinner; perhaps there's a new Thai restaurant you've wanted to try. Get involved in your community or with your school's PTO. It's a great way to make new friends.

☀ **90** Spend Time with Yourself

It's impossible to nourish your spirit if you don't pay attention to who you truly are within. But how do you do that? How do you get to the core of your being?

One of the easiest ways to do this is to simply spend time with your spirit. For me, the best time to do this is in the morning before I get out of bed or at night before I go to sleep. I close my eyes and let go of negativity, stress, or anything else that is holding my spirit prison.

How do you let go of negativity? Start by concentrating on something that makes you happy. Now stop thinking about all those things that build up in your mind all day long. For instance, forget about the report that's due in the morning, stop worrying about your kids' crazy schedules, and those bills that have yet to be paid. This is your time and you are allowed to concentrate only on you.

Once I have cleansed my thoughts, I spend the next fifteen to thirty minutes focusing on myself and the feelings within. This is actually the best time for me to focus on new ideas for books and everything else that I write because I am now fresh and open to new ideas.

☀ 91 Don't Try to be Perfect

These days many people spend so much needless time trying to be perfect in a world that has little patience for imperfection. We want to have the perfect body, the ideal family, the great career, the big beautiful house in the suburbs, etc. My question is this: Why? You're not perfect and neither is anyone else.

Just be yourself and realize that you are the only one who can decide what is perfect or not perfect in your life.

☀ 92 Do Something Unexpected for Someone

I once fractured my tailbone when I fell down a full flight of steps. Needless to say, I was in a lot of pain and out of commission for about two weeks. The morning after my fall, my doorbell rang and in came my loyal friend Christina bearing enough food for a week, complete with rice pudding (my favorite) and her husband John's homemade wine.

I was just overwhelmed with her unexpected act of kindness, love, and generosity. My back was hurting like hell, but at that moment, I actually felt great. It was so heartwarming to know that Christina would go out of her way to do something like that for me.

I did not have to worry about cooking dinner for a week, but more importantly, I realized how blessed I was to have such a wonderful friend. And Christina knows that I would do the same for her.

☀ 93 Volunteer For a Cause

Volunteering your time takes doing something nice for someone to the next level. In most cases, you will not even know the person or people you have volunteered to help.

Statistics show more than 50 percent of Americans volunteer annually for various causes. A well-known example is the Susan B. Komen Race for the Cure which sponsors various 5K walks in several cities to raise money for the fight against breast cancer.

The satisfaction and joy that you receive far outweigh the time and effort that you give when volunteering. You may meet new people, learn new skills, or travel to places you've never been before. And, of course, you will feel needed and content knowing that your efforts can help to bring happiness to someone else.

☀ 94 Screen Your Worries

If I had a dime for every time I've worried about something, I'd be a very wealthy woman. It's natural to worry at times. The problem, though, is that most of our worries are about things that have a minute chance of ever happening.

I have a friend who prefers to travel by car because she constantly worries about being in a plane crash. The odds of being killed in a plane crash are said to be one-in-twenty-five million while the odds of being killed in a car crash are one-in-five thousand. Americans have the constant habit of protecting themselves against perceived dangers while leaving themselves open to real ones.

As another example, we worry about the minuscule possibility of mad cow pathogen being in our beef yet most of us don't stop to consider that the cholesterol can lead to heart disease—the leading cause of death in the United States.

☀ 95 Fill Your Mind with Positives

You can either boost or dampen your spirit just by what you choose to expose yourself to. My husband often wonders why I won't allow myself to watch horror movies. He chuckles every time I cover my eyes when something bad is about to happen on TV. I don't like watching these depressing films because I don't want to fill my head with all those frightening images. I want to watch things that will make me feel good inside.

The same thing can be said for the company that you keep or the newspaper articles that you read. If you expose yourself to negative images, you will think negatively and feel down. Instead, watch a movie that will make you laugh or read a book that will lift your spirit.

☀ 96 Make Time for Your Friends

I cannot even imagine where I would be today if it weren't for my friends. They are the ones that I so often call when I need love and support or even when I just need to vent. They lift my spirit when I'm down and steer me in the right direction when I feel lost. We don't all see each other as much as we would like, but we make every effort to spend time together whether it's for a quick cup of coffee downtown or a relaxing margarita on the patio. It doesn't matter what we do as long as we do it together.

Don't get so tied up in the daily rat race of life that you deprive yourself of the company of your friends. If you just don't have the time for whatever reason, pick up the phone and let them know that you still care.

☀ 97 Don't Try to Change Others

If you've ever tried to change someone, you know it doesn't work. So if you're trying to change someone right now, stop. It's a wasted effort. No one can change unless he wants to and no one will want to change unless he recognizes the need to do so.

The only person you can change is yourself. Rather than spending wasted time trying to change others, use that much-needed energy to help yourself.

☀ 98 Live Longer . . . Get a Pet

Most people are quick to note the constant companionship and unconditional love that having a pet can provide. Few, however, realize that this love also comes with a host of health and psychological benefits. In fact, studies have shown that dog owners actually make fewer visits to the hospital and tend to live longer.

Pets help to boost our spirit in so many ways. Remember, they don't judge us the way that people sometimes do. They make us feel better, thereby reducing stress levels and helping to reduce blood pressure. And let's not forget that we need to take our four-legged friends for walks. So having a dog encourages us to get out and walk, one of the best forms of exercise.

Owning a pet is certainly not for everyone. But for most people, the many benefits of having a pet far outweigh the added responsibility and work.

☀ 99 Treat Yourself

Whenever my spirit needs a lift, I usually take myself to the mall. I love to treat myself and buy something. It could be something as simple as new nail polish or as extravagant as a new Coach purse. But the important thing is that I buy something just for me.

Buying something new at the mall may not work for you. Perhaps your idea of a treat is hiring a babysitter and going out for a nice romantic dinner with your partner or a much-needed trip to the spa. Whatever makes you feel good, just do it! Treat yourself.

☀ 100 "Dance to the Music"

Recently, when I was having one of my "bad" days, my four-year-old daughter Lia tugged on my arm and said, "Come on, Mommy, dance to the music." Then she proceeded to sing and dance around to this upbeat children's song ("Dance to the Music" by the Wiggles). As I watched her, I felt all my negative energy leave my body as a smile engulfed my face and I began to laugh.

Before I knew it, I was dancing and singing around the house with Lia and my oldest daughter Erica. And the best part is when I dance, it is impossible for me not to smile. Try it. You'll have a great time.

☀ 101 Read, Read, Read

Reading is by far one of my favorite pastimes. Depending on the nature of what I am reading, I relax and become completely engulfed in the story. Since my mind is busy absorbing everything, there's no room for me to take in negative thoughts or worry about everyday problems.

Plus, I've never read a book that hasn't taught me something. Even if you dislike the book, I'm sure there is something you can learn from it. This book is a perfect example. As we approach the end of this book, what have you learned? Has it made you feel better in some ways? I hope so.

☀ **102** Don't Live Your Life in Fear

The events of September 11 were life changing for many. But the truth is we can't live our lives in fear. First, that's exactly what terrorists want us to do. Second, by living our lives in fear, we stop living. We are allowing negative thoughts to take over our future and control our day-to-day lives. And finally, we fear something that may never happen.

As the saying goes, we have nothing to fear except fear itself. Live your life happily and make the most of every day.

☀ **103** Have a Little Faith

I'm not trying to preach religion here. What I am saying is that we all have a need to believe in something. We need to believe that there is a higher being out there somewhere watching over us. It doesn't matter whether you are Catholic, Jewish, Muslim, or Protestant.

Whether you choose to follow the path of traditional religion or that of science, there are many roads to faith in today's society. By choosing your belief system, you will have a better understanding of both who you are and the world around you.

☀ **104** Don't Care What Others Say

When I was in high school, one of my classmates nicknamed me "The Hedge." This was extremely insulting because I have very thick, coarse curly hair. I would walk down the hallway on my way to another class, and she would yell out, "The Hedge is coming." Needless to say, this was hurtful and embarrassing.

Others picked on me either because of the way that I walked or because I suffered from hearing loss. Back then, I did not know how to handle this. I became very upset and cried tears of anger and disappointment. I couldn't believe people would be so cruel.

That was thankfully a long time ago. Today, I don't care what people say about me. It makes no difference what others think. I know and accept who I am and that's all that matters. Once you learn to love yourself just the way you are, you can become connected and truly happy with your inner self.

☀ 105 Give Someone the Benefit of the Doubt

In October 2009, I lost a dear friend to lung cancer. Natalie and I came to know each other while I was doing research for my book *Visits from Heaven*. She not only wrote the preface for my book, but she also put me in contact with several contributors. She was a blessing beyond words.

Natalie had also agreed to be part of the sequel *Visits to Heaven*, but for no apparent reason, I stopped hearing from her. My e-mails and phone calls went unanswered. At first, I assumed that she was just busy, but then I became angry and began to feel slighted. After all, I reasoned, why couldn't she just pick up the phone and call me?

She didn't return my phone calls or respond to my e-mails because as I later found out she was dying from Stage 4 lung cancer. The disease took swift control of her body and within thirteen months after her diagnosis, she was gone. Her husband explained that she didn't say anything to me and others because she wanted us to remember her as she was—alive and well.

I can't imagine the strength and courage that it must have taken for my friend to keep quiet about everything that she had to endure. Her death taught me a very hard lesson. Don't just assume; always give someone the benefit of the doubt.

Marci Shimoff

Is This a Friendly Universe?

WE ARE IN THE midst of truly amazing times. I believe that our desire to experience lasting happiness at a deeper level of our consciousness is an indication of a time of global awakening. Experiencing this profound state of genuine happiness starts by first recognizing how the two basic energies in life, *contraction and expansion*, affect us.

Everything in the universe, including you, is composed of energy, and everything you do either expands or contracts your energy. When you experience happiness, your energy expands, but your energy contracts when you are unhappy. Being in a state of expansion allows you to live from the soul or your higher self, realizing the essence of who you truly are. However, when you are in a state of contraction, you are living from your ego or "small self." It is the ego that feels threatened, believes there is much to be feared, and resists the flow of life and "what is."

Since the release of phenomenally successful book and film, *The Se-*

cret, there has been a lot of buzz about the Law of Attraction. Simply stated, the Law of Attraction says that we draw to ourselves like a magnet whatever is in energetic alignment with our thoughts, words, feelings and actions. In other words, like attracts like; what you appreciate, appreciates. Whenever you appreciate the happiness that already exists in your life, you attract more of it into your life. Likewise, when you come from negativity or fear, you attract more of that into your life.

This is a wonderful principle. However, many people attempt to use the Law of Attraction to draw in the "things" they believe will make them happy. Unfortunately, this is backwards. While we think that success and getting the things we want will bring us happiness, it's actually happiness that will bring us success. Happiness is the foundation of the Law of Attraction

How, then, can we be happy right now? By using a wonderful three-step formula for applying the Law of Attraction to experience greater happiness I first learned about this simple process through my coach, performance consultant Bill Levacy. Here is how it works:

1. Intention: Be clear about what you want to create. Set your intention on experiencing greater happiness in your life.

2. Attention: What you focus on grows, so put your attention (your thoughts, words, feelings, and actions) on that which supports your inner peace and well-being.

3. No Tension: Relax, let go, and trust that the benevolent universe is always bringing you your highest good.

That third step is essential, though it can be tricky for many people. Einstein once said that the most important question a person can ask himself is, "Is this a friendly universe?" As part of the research I conducted for my book, *Happy for No Reason*, I interviewed over 100 unconditionally happy people, and I found that they all answered Einstein's question with a resounding, "YES!"

Rather than thinking that the universe is out to get them, happy people believe the universe is out to support them. No matter what challenge they face, they see the events in their lives through the lens of benevolence, choosing to believe that "ultimately, this is happening for my good. There are no mistakes. Let me look for the blessing and the gift in this." This belief in a friendly universe is the basis of their relaxed and trusting attitude in life.

Research shows that a belief in a friendly universe can actually impact a person's health. A study conducted by Gail Ironson, PhD, MD, professor of Psychology and Psychiatry at the University of Miami, found that people with HIV who believed in a loving universal power remained healthier longer than people who believed in a universal power that was punishing.

This may be a hard concept to swallow. Certainly there are many horrible things that happen in this world: war, persecution, famine, and suffering. It's easy to think that we don't live in a friendly universe. The one thing that has helped me embrace the idea that the universe is always out to support me is the knowledge that all the wise men and women who have ever lived, the sages and saints of the past and present, have shared this belief. I've also seen that people who are Happy for No Reason use this as a guiding principle, and you can use it yourself to raise your own happiness level.

Rather than trying to decide whether this principle is true or not, I suggest that you adopt this perspective for the next few weeks and see how different your life feels. That means that whatever happens, assume that the universe is on your side—even if it isn't obvious to you in the beginning. Look for the lessons and the gifts in each experience.

When I first began doing this myself, I noticed that although I wasn't jumping up and down with joy and loving everything that happened in my life, I definitely felt a lot more ease and peace inside. When you believe that the universe is out to support you, you can stop resisting what is happening. This doesn't mean being passive or complacent about the events in the world or in your own life. It simply means not fighting or bemoaning what has already happened and can't be changed.

Many of us spend a tremendous amount of energy being upset and resisting life. But when you take the view that there are no mistakes and accept what is, you can use your energy instead to deal effectively with the situation now. Try it and see. You've got nothing to lose but your angst. And I guarantee your happiness level will soar when you realize you do live in a friendly universe after all!

About Marci Shimoff

As the woman's face of the biggest self-help book phenomenon in history, *Chicken Soup for the Soul,* Marci Shimoff is one of the bestselling female nonfiction authors of all time. Her books, including *Chicken Soup for the Woman's Soul* and *Chicken Soup for the Mother's Soul* have sold more than fourteen million copies worldwide. Marci is also a featured teacher in the international film and book sensation, *The Secret.*

Her newest book, *HAPPY FOR NO REASON: 7 Steps to Being Happy from the Inside Out,* offers a revolutionary approach to experiencing deep and lasting happiness. It immediately soared to the top of many bestseller lists, including the *New York Times, Wall Street Journal,* and Amazon.com bestseller lists, and has been translated into thirty-one languages.

A celebrated transformational leader and a leading expert on happiness, success, and the Law of Attraction, Marci has inspired millions of people around the world, sharing her breakthrough methods for personal fulfillment and professional success. Marci earned her MBA from UCLA. For more information on Marci Shimoff, please visit www.happyfornoreason.com

Edgar Cayce . . .
The Healing Power of the Mind

PSYCHOLOGISTS, MYSTICS, PHYSICISTS, AND philosophers alike have been attempting to bridge the gap between attitude and reality for centuries. One of the best known is Edgar Cayce who was once deemed "the world's most mysterious man" and is today recognized as America's greatest psychic. Throughout his life, he was an active member of the Disciples of Christ and pledged to read the *Bible* once a year until his death. Because of his faith, Cayce is said to have agonized over his psychic abilities. While in a self-induced trance state, he was able to answer questions on everything from the beginning of existence to spirituality and health.

Once, while suffering from severe laryngitis, Cayce lost his voice and sought the help of a hypnotist. While in a hypnotic trance, he was also able to describe the nature of his sickness and diagnose a cure. The loss of his voice, he noted, was due to psychological paralysis and could be cured by increasing blood volume in the voice box area. The hypnotist is said to have asked for the blood flow in this area to be increased and, incredibly, upon awakening his voice was restored.

During his lifetime, Cayce performed over 14,000 readings. Over 8,000 additional readings were said to have been performed but not recorded. Although thousands of his predictions were proven to be accurate, he considered his medical readings and healings to be the most crucial part of his work. Through his readings, Cayce was able to correctly diagnose and in many cases cure a variety of illnesses. For example, a blind man is said to have regained part of his vision in one eye by following Cayce's medical advice.

In most cases, Cayce was not with his subjects at the time that the readings occurred. He remained in his trance state while lying on his couch and needed only to know the subject's name, address, and where the person was at the time of the reading. The unconscious mind, he noted, has access to a wealth of information not available to the conscious mind.

His healings were so astounding that a hospital in his name was founded in 1928. He would go on to diagnose many more illnesses before his death in 1945. He did so, he often explained, by connecting the illnesses to both the mental and emotional well-being of his patients. In other words, in order to treat physical ailments, you must also consider the mind, body, and spirit. All three are interconnected, each affecting the other. Any form of dysfunction in any area will affect our entire well-being.

Any negative change in our attitude (anger, sadness, resentment, etc.) can change our nervous system, thereby affecting our entire body and even lead to disease. The mind (which Cayce noted was totally separate from the brain) uses the brain and the nervous system to maintain the mind–body–spirit interface. Calling worry and fear the greatest enemies, he said, "For thoughts are things. And they have their effect upon individuals, just as physical as sticking a pin in the hand."

All three (mind, body, and spirit) must be balanced for the body to be able to heal itself. If a person's attitude is in complete alignment with his body (organs, nervous system, etc.), then Cayce went as far as saying, "For, as may be told by any pathologist, there is no known reason why any individual entity should not live as long as it desires. And there is no death, save in thy consciousness. Because all others have died, ye expect to, and you do!"

He pointed out that the proper function of the endocrine system is crucial to a person's ability to prolong his life span. These glands serve as the conduit between the nervous system and the soul.

Our emotions, he explained, affect what happens to these glands.

Just by being angry, we can cause toxins to be released from the glands. "No one can hate his neighbor and not have stomach or liver trouble. No one can be jealous and allow the anger of same and not have upset digestion or heart disorder."

Edgar Cayce repeatedly spoke of what he called "mind as the builder." Simply put, whatever we believe, our mind will build. Belief and anticipation, he felt, play a crucial role in the healing process. The following are examples of Cayce's readings pertaining to the relationship between our attitude and physical well being:

1. And that about the body that keeps the cheery mental attitude, in the way and manner as of companion - as has been given often. Cheery companionship is WONDERFUL for the body; yet this, as is seen at times, may be overdone - but those companionships that are in the manner kept in the way as has been outlined prove effectual and prove beneficial. These are necessary attributes toward the betterment of the physical forces of this body.   106-18

2. Keep in the attitude of creative forces. Keep happy. Do not let anxiety of any nature disturb. For it will have much to do with the nature or character of the individual dependent upon the body.   23-16

3. In this there is presented, as is seen from the experiences of the body conscious and the mental consciousness of the entity, through the subconscious those projections of physical conditions and mental positions or manifestations that bring to the body-conscious mind this condition. It is as the warning that the mental attitude and the body-conscious mind must gain a different concept of conditions being presented, that the full consciousness of the entity may not feel that this condition of paralysis to the mental portion of the entity, or that such conditions in the mental development, is at the standstill, or must be broken; else, as is seen, there is the call to that consciousness to whom the body conscious and the mental consciousness of the

individual turns for the instruction, see?   136-39

4. In the physical, we find there are physical attributes in the body that are abnormal for the body and these may be corrected through spiritual and mental attitude, as well as through the physical conditions that bear relation one to another.   180-1

In the book, *Edgar Cayce on Healing Foods for Body, Mind and Spirit,* author William A. McGarey, MD explains, "Getting rid of a cancer is not simply removal of the group of cells that are apparently causing the difficulty. It means correcting the basic cause of the problem—whether it be attitudes, circulation, neurology, acid–alkaline balance, or whatever—and changing the physiology of the body so that it functions constructively, not in a destructive manner to bring death to the body. This is the manner in which Cayce saw the forces of the body acting, always related to emotions, stresses, attitudes, and the belief patterns of the unconscious mind."

On January 1, 1945, Cayce said that he would be buried four days later. He died on January 3 and was buried two days later. Ironically, his last prophecy was the foretelling of his own death at the age of sixty-seven. The Association for Research and Enlightenment, Inc. (A.R.E.) in Virginia Beach, Virginia was founded in 1931 and to this day continues to be the headquarters for the preservation of Edgar Cayce's work.

When asked about the mind's creation of reality, Cayce concluded, "The spirit is life. The mind is the builder. The physical is the result."

The Act of Forgiveness

DURING THE QUESTION AND answer session of one of my presenta-
tions, a woman raised her hand and shyly asked, "What do you do if
you have a friend who is always negative and you no longer feel good
around her?" That's easy, I replied, "Forgive yourself and your friend
and let go."

She looked at me be perplexed and asked, "I can understand why I
need to forgive her but why do I need to forgive me?" I looked at her
and replied, "Because you are the one that needs to let go and you need
not feel guilty about doing so."

Webster's defines forgiveness as the act of renouncing anger or resentment against someone. There's no one definition but, in general,
forgiveness means to let go. We've all been hurt or mistreated by the
actions or words of another person. These hurtful acts can create lasting
wounds not easily healed.

Although forgiveness offers us instant gratification and happiness, it
can be difficult when those who have wronged us don't seem to deserve our forgiveness in the first place. We can be hurt in so many ways:
betrayal, physical abuse, rudeness are just a few. Forgiveness is easier
said than done because it is not possible without first letting go of the
resentments of the past. But what most people don't realize is forgiveness benefits the forgiver more than the wrongdoer. When we choose
not to forgive and to carry resentment, we cause all kinds of havoc to
our emotional well-being.

When we do choose to forgive, it is possible to start anew and almost become a completely different person. In the film *Ray* directed by Taylor Hackford, Jamie Foxx plays award-winning singer Ray Charles. In the movie, Ray finally quits using heroin after realizing that his little brother's death was not his fault. (Ray saw his brother drown in a wash pail and was never able to forgive himself feeling that he should have been able to do something). Once he is able to forgive himself, he no longer feels the need to use drugs and totally turns his life around.

Those who forgive live happier and healthier lives while those who don't suffer from a multitude of health issues, including stress, high-blood pressure, and heart disease. On the other hand, the opposite is true for those who choose to practice forgiveness. This group recurrently benefits from reduced emotional pain and a sense of peace and happiness.

At times, forgiveness is not easy, but the rewards are always great. It is our ego that causes us to either not forgive or forgive but not forget. Some believe this is just another way of not forgiving. Sydney J. Harris made mention of this when he said, "There's no point in burying the hatchet if you're going to put up a marker on the site."

While I understand why some feel this way, I can't say I agree. Forgiving does not mean the same thing as forgetting. The hurtful act that a loved one committed against you may forever be a part of your memory. Realistically, for example, how can we forget when a partner has committed adultery? To me, this is just not possible. What is possible is to lessen the grip of this hurtful act by practicing forgiveness.

Forgiving means closure and letting go of the past. If you don't do so, you will continue to be stuck in the past and will be unable to experience your true nature. But this doesn't mean all is forgotten.

Again, happiness is impossible without forgiveness. The burden and weight of resentments is just much too great. Yet it is still so difficult for many of us because forgiveness is perceived as giving in. So if you don't feel that you did any wrong, how can you give in? Others feel that giving in means we deem the other person's behavior acceptable. Simply put, the benefits are greater for the forgiver and it does not mean the other person's ill behavior was acceptable. It just means that you are willing to look passed it.

The people closest to us are the most likely to hurt us. One reason for this is the fact that they are the ones that we love and trust. No matter who hurts you, it is best to deal with the situation as quickly as possible. The longer things are left unresolved, the more grudges, resentment, and anger will come to the surface taking the place of any positive feelings you may have had for this person.

It is important to note, however, that it is never too late to embrace forgiveness. It just becomes more difficult as more and more time passes. Everyone deals with hurt and forgiveness in different ways. One step is to ask yourself if you are willing to lose a relationship over the wrongful act that was committed. If you answer is no, then move toward reconciliation.

If your answer is truly yes and you cannot get passed what took place, you still need to practice forgiveness. As I said before, you will need to forgive and let go. Regardless of whether this person will or will not be a part of your life, you need to forgive him or her so that you don't harbor any ill feelings within.

Buddhism has long believed that feelings of hatred and anger have long-term effects on our karma. It is not the victimizer but the victim who is more of the unfortunate one in this case. My favorite quote about forgiveness was written by English poet Alexander Pope. "To err is human; to forgive, divine."

A Course in Miracles teaches that forgiveness is not just about letting go of bitterness but awakening to our true nature. In so doing, we realize that there is nothing to forgive because unjust separation is not actually real. Forgiveness, then, removes the blocks to seeing only goodness within others.

Final Thoughts

"A man is but the product of his thoughts; what he thinks, he becomes."   Mohandas Gandhi

ACCORDING TO DR. RICHARD Gillett, we can change our reality simply by changing our beliefs. In his book, *Change Your Mind, Change Your World*, he explains that self-fulfilling prophecies have three basic steps:

Belief creates action
Action creates reaction or result
Reaction or result confirms belief.

He goes on to say, "If you're afraid a dog will bite you, it is more likely to bite you." Your beliefs or your thoughts force you to react in a certain way. Your actions therefore create the end result. I bring this up in conclusion to this book because making up your mind to be happy is only the beginning. The next step, as Dr. Gillett, notes is action and reaction.

You are not bound by the circumstances of your life. You can change your life simply by changing the way you think. You can change your life then by how you react to your thoughts. Each day as you live your life, choose to focus on the things that will bring you happiness; choose to see the good in everything, and believe in your ability to make things happen.

Happiness lies within you. The outside world is not the cause of your unhappiness. You are the cause. What you experience is the result of the way you think. But the good news is because you are in control of your destiny; you can change your world.

In this book, I have shared 105 simple tips that can help you change the way you think and go back to your true nature, but the truth is none of it will do you any good unless your actions follow in pursuit. You need to have no doubt in the sheer power of your actions. You are the world and the world is you. Everything that you see is a reflection of the way you think.

When I was little, I had great difficulty looking at myself in the mirror. All I could see was this little girl with kinky hair and an overbite who walked and talked funny. And since this is what I saw, this was, in fact, what everyone else saw. I was constantly picked on and felt as though true happiness was never quite within reach. How could I expect others to accept me for who I was when I didn't accept who I was?

Today, I no longer think of myself as that little girl. Yes, I am a woman who happens to have a disability. But I am so much more than that. It took me a long time to realize that my negative thoughts were, in fact, starting to manifest themselves as acts in my play of life. It would have been the longest running play of all time had I not decided to lower the curtains and direct a new play.

Changing my thoughts has changed my life in so many ways. But nothing would have happened had I not made a choice. Happiness is within all of us but the role it will play is our choice. When asked about proof of one's existence, the great French philosopher and mathematician René Descartes responded, "Cogito, ergo sum" (I think, therefore I am). Our very being depends on the contents of our mind.

May you always focus on the beautiful and then reap the rewards as the beautiful begins to manifest around you.

My PT Journal

IN THIS BOOK, I discussed the use of verbal affirmations and positive thoughts to lift our spirit and change our moods for the better. Many, including me, believe this is so because of the Law of Attraction which basically states that we experience the manifestation of our thoughts and feelings. In other words, like attracts like. If we think negatively, we attract negatives into our lives. And if we think positively, we attract positive experiences.

Have you ever awoken in the morning in a bad mood and then found that the whole day seemed to follow in pursuit? Everything seems to go wrong. Well, the good news is you have the power to change your day and your life by simply thinking positively. In fact, I am so sure of this theory that I am including a "PT (Positive Thoughts) Journal" that follows.

Keep this book on your nightstand within easy reach. Each morning before you get out of bed, concentrate on something positive. Perhaps it's a special friend in your life. Close your eyes and visualize this person. Give thanks that this person is in your life and then take a moment to record your thoughts in your PT Journal. For example, you might write, "I am blessed to have Amy in my life. She makes me laugh." Each day challenge yourself to reflect on more positive thoughts and record them in your PT Journal.

Your entries can be big or small. You might say "I am grateful for my beautiful and healthy children" or simply "I am glad I had a great meal yesterday." The problem is that we become so accustomed to things in our lives that we forget to be appreciative of what we already have. The challenge, though, is not just being grateful for the good things in your life but finding the good in the bad. The most powerful entries are ones that transform a negative situation into a positive one.

As I said earlier in this book, I was born with a disability, but I choose not to look at the negatives of the situation. Instead, I am grateful for the strong, determined person I have become because of it.

How many times have you thought, "I hate my job? It's so stressful. I wish I could quit." Now, I'd like you to change that to "I am grateful to have a job while so many others are out of work." Even in the case of death, we can think of a positive. Of course, you will experience sadness. But at the same time, ask yourself, "Did not the death of this person allow me to spend time with my family and friends? Did it not remind me once again how precious life truly is?" The situation is the same; the only difference is the response.

If mornings don't work for you, pick a time that does and stick to it. Commit to a time everyday and use it. You will be amazed at how many positive thoughts you will collect. Whenever your mood needs a lift, go back and read your PT Journal. I guarantee you that it will lift your spirit and change your life.

After reading this book and writing in your PT Journal for at least two weeks, retake the PPF Test on the following page to see if your happiness level has changed.

The Final Happiness PPF Test

TEST YOUR HAPPINESS *PPF LEVEL

I am happy.
Less True   ☺   ☺   ☺   ☺   ☺   More True

I focus on the positive in any situation.
Less True   ☺   ☺   ☺   ☺   ☺   More True

I say I love you at least once a day.
Less True   ☺   ☺   ☺   ☺   ☺   More True

I make time for friends and family.
Less True   ☺   ☺   ☺   ☺   ☺   More True

My life is purposeful.
Less True   ☺   ☺   ☺   ☺   ☺   More True

I accept the past.
Less True   ☺   ☺   ☺   ☺   ☺   More True

I am optimistic about the future.
Less True   ☺   ☺   ☺   ☺   ☺   More True

I can do anything I put my mind to.
Less True   ☺   ☺   ☺   ☺   ☺   More True

I give hugs as often as I can.
Less True   ☺   ☺   ☺   ☺   ☺   More True

I am honest with myself and the way I feel.
Less True   ☺   ☺   ☺   ☺   ☺   More True

I seek out positive people.
Less True   ☺   ☺   ☺   ☺   ☺   More True

I weed out the people who drag me down.
Less True   ☺   ☺   ☺   ☺   ☺   More True

I wake up with a positive thought every morning.
Less True   ☺   ☺   ☺   ☺   ☺   More True

I believe everything happens for a reason.
Less True   ☺   ☺   ☺   ☺   ☺   More True

I have fun often enough.
Less True   ☺   ☺   ☺   ☺   ☺   More True

I deserve to be happy.
Less True   ☺   ☺   ☺   ☺   ☺   More True

I accept myself for who I am.
Less True   ☺   ☺   ☺   ☺   ☺   More True

It doesn't matter what others think of me.
Less True   ☺   ☺   ☺   ☺   ☺   More True

This world is a beautiful place.
Less True   ☺   ☺   ☺   ☺   ☺   More True

I smile often.
Less True   ☺   ☺   ☺   ☺   ☺   More True

I surprise my friends for no reason.
Less True   ☺   ☺   ☺   ☺   ☺   More True

I am fun to be around.
Less True   ☺   ☺   ☺   ☺   ☺   More True

I don't worry about things I have no control over.
Less True　☺　☺　☺　☺　☺　More True

I am exactly where I should be in life.
Less True　☺　☺　☺　☺　☺　More True

I laugh just because it makes me feel good.
Less True　☺　☺　☺　☺　☺　More True

I appreciate my old friends and am always open to making new ones.
Less True　☺　☺　☺　☺　☺　More True

I can easily forgive others.
Less True　☺　☺　☺　☺　☺　More True

I am a good person and always try to help others.
Less True　☺　☺　☺　☺　☺　More True

*PPF refers to being accepting of the PAST, actively happy in the PRESENT, and optimistic about the FUTURE.

 **My PT Journal Pages**

In him there are no limitations; one only limits self by doubt or fear. Edgar Cayce Reading 2574-1

Those who wish to sing always find a song. **Swedish proverb**

_____

_____

_____

_____

_____

_____

_____

_____

_____

_____

_____

_____

_____

_____

_____

_____

_____

_____

_____

_____

_____

_____

_____

_____

_____

_____

_____

_____

_____

_____

_____

_____

_____

_____

_____

_____

_____

_____

_____

_____

_____

For, he that expects nothing shall not be disappointed, but he that expects much—if he lives and uses that in hand day by day—shall be full to running over. Edgar Cayce Reading 557-3

_____

_____

_____

_____

_____

_____

_____

_____

_____

_____

_____

_____

_____

_____

_____

_____

_____

_____

If you are not getting as much from life as you want to, then examine the state of your enthusiasm. **Norman Vincent Peale**

_____

_____

_____

_____

_____

_____

_____

_____

_____

_____

_____

_____

_____

_____

_____

_____

There is progress whether ye are going forward or backward! The thing is to move!   *Edgar Cayce Reading 3027-2*

_____

_____

_____

_____

_____

_____

_____

_____

_____

_____

_____

_____

_____

_____

_____

_____

_____

_____

Our greatest glory is not in never falling but in rising every time we fall.   *Confucius*

_____

_____

_____

_____

_____

_____

_____

_____

_____

_____

_____

_____

_____

_____

_____

_____

_____

_____

Know this: that whatever situation you find yourself in, it is what is necessary for your development. Edgar Cayce Reading 2998-2

_____

_____

_____

_____

_____

_____

_____

_____

_____

_____

_____

_____

_____

_____

_____

_____

_____

Everything has its wonders, even darkness and silence, and I learn whatever state I may be in, therein to be content.   *Helen Keller*

Analyze thy life's experiences, see thy shortcomings, see thy virtues.
Minimize those faults, magnify and glorify thy virtues.
Edgar Cayce Reading 2524-3

_____

_____

_____

_____

_____

_____

_____

_____

_____

_____

_____

_____

_____

_____

_____

Nothing great was ever achieved without enthusiasm.
Ralph Waldo Emerson

_____

_____

_____

_____

_____

_____

_____

_____

_____

_____

_____

_____

_____

_____

_____

_____

Then, what is destiny? That the soul who seeks shall the sooner find; that the soul who puts into practice day by day that which is known may the sooner enjoin itself to that which is hope and peace and happiness and love and joy in the earth. Edgar Cayce Reading 262-77

_____

_____

_____

_____

_____

_____

_____

_____

_____

_____

_____

_____

_____

_____

_____

_____

_____

_____

It was a high counsel that once heard given to a young person, "Always do what you are afraid to do."   *Ralph Waldo Emerson*

_____

_____

_____

_____

_____

_____

_____

_____

_____

_____

_____

_____

_____

_____

_____

_____

_____

_____

_____

_____

_____

_____

_____

_____

_____

_____

_____

_____

_____

_____

_____

_____

_____

_____

_____

_____

_____

_____

_____

Try in thine own experience, each; that ye speak not for one whole day unkindly of any; that ye say not a harsh word to any, about any; and see what a day would bring to you the next lesson, happiness. Edgar Cayce Reading 262-106

_____

_____

_____

_____

_____

_____

_____

_____

_____

_____

_____

_____

_____

_____

_____

_____

_____

_____

The best way out is always through. Robert Frost

_____

_____

_____

_____

_____

_____

_____

_____

_____

_____

_____

_____

_____

_____

_____

_____

_____

_____

For it is only those who know divine love that know Happiness.
Edgar Cayce Reading 262-109

_____

_____

_____

_____

_____

_____

_____

_____

_____

_____

_____

_____

_____

_____

_____

_____

_____

_____

Happiness is not a station you arrive at, but a manner of traveling.
Margaret B. Runbeck

_____

_____

_____

_____

_____

_____

_____

_____

_____

_____

_____

_____

_____

_____

_____

_____

About the Author

Josie Varga is the author of *Visits from Heaven* and *Footprints in the Sand: A Disabled Woman's Inspiring Journey to Happiness*. Besides being a former communications consultant, she has also served as the director of communications and editor for a trade association. As a motivational speaker, she encourages others to focus on the positive by choosing to be happy.

Her next publication, due out in January 2011, is *Visits to Heaven*—an unparalleled book which highlights near-death experiences from around the globe and includes testimony from some of the world's leading experts in NDEs. She also has several other book projects in the works.

In addition to her book writing, she has completed several treatments for reality television including a television series for her book *Visits from Heaven*. A creative thinker, Josie is the holder of two patents. She lives in Westfield, New Jersey, with her husband John and daughters Erica and Lia.

For more information about the author, please visit her at www.josievarga.com. You may also contact Josie through her Web site; she loves to hear from her readers.

4TH DIMENSION PRESS

An Imprint of A.R.E. Press

4th Dimension Press is an imprint of A.R.E. Press, the publishing division of Edgar Cayce's Association for Research and Enlightenment (A.R.E.).

We publish books, DVDs, and CDs in the fields of intuition, psychic abilities, ancient mysteries, philosophy, comparative religious studies, personal and spiritual development, and holistic health.

For more information, or to receive a catalog, contact us by mail, phone, or online at:

4th Dimension Press
215 67th Street, Virginia Beach, VA 23451-2061
800-333-4499

4THDIMENSIONPRESS.COM

EDGAR CAYCE'S A.R.E.

What Is A.R.E.?

The Association for Research and Enlightenment, Inc., (A.R.E.®) was founded in 1931 to research and make available information on psychic development, dreams, holistic health, meditation, and life after death. As an open-membership research organization, the A.R.E. continues to study and publish such information, to initiate research, and to promote conferences, distance learning, and regional events. Edgar Cayce, the most documented psychic of our time, was the moving force in the establishment of A.R.E.

Who Was Edgar Cayce?

Edgar Cayce (1877-1945) was born on a farm near Hopkinsville, Ky. He was an average individual in most respects. Yet, throughout his life, he manifested one of the most remarkable psychic talents of all time. As a young man, he found that he was able to enter into a self-induced trance state, which enabled him to place his mind in contact with an unlimited source of information. While asleep, he could answer questions or give accurate discourses on any topic. These discourses, more than 14,000 in number, were transcribed as he spoke and are called "readings."

Given the name and location of an individual anywhere in the world, he could correctly describe a person's condition and outline a regimen of treatment. The consistent accuracy of his diagnoses and the effectiveness of the treatments he prescribed made him a medical phenomenon, and he came to be called the "father of holistic medicine."

Eventually, the scope of Cayce's readings expanded to include such subjects as world religions, philosophy, psychology, parapsychology, dreams, history, the missing years of Jesus, ancient civilizations, soul growth, psychic development, prophecy, and reincarnation.

A.R.E. Membership

People from all walks of life have discovered meaningful and life-transforming insights through membership in A.R.E. To learn more about Edgar Cayce's A.R.E. and how membership in the A.R.E. can enhance your life, visit our Web site at EdgarCayce.org, or call us toll-free at 800-333-4499.

Edgar Cayce's A.R.E.
215 67th Street, Virginia Beach, VA 23451-2061

EDGARCAYCE.ORG